Tide Rips &
Back Eddies

Tide Rips &

Back Eddies

Bill Proctor's Tales
of Blackfish Sound

Bill Proctor &
Yvonne Maximchuk

HARBOUR
PUBLISHING

HARBOUR PUBLISHING CO. LTD.
PO Box 219, Madeira Park, BC, VON 2H0
www.harbourpublishing.com

Cover painting and interior drawings by Yvonne Maximchuk
Bill Proctor author photo by Yvonne Maximchuk
Yvonne Maximchuk author photo by Albert Munro
Map by Roger Handling
Edited by Pam Robertson
Indexed by Kyla Shauer
Cover design by Daniela Hajdukovic
Text design by Shed Simas
Printed and bound in Canada
Printed on FSC-certified paper

Harbour Publishing acknowledges the support of the Canada Council for the Arts,
which last year invested $157 million to bring the arts to Canadians throughout the
country. We also gratefully acknowledge financial support from the Government of
Canada through the Canada Book Fund and from the Province of British Columbia
through the BC Arts Council and the Book Publishing Tax Credit.

CATALOGUING DATA AVAILABLE FROM LIBRARY AND ARCHIVES CANADA
ISBN 978-1-55017-725-1 (paper)
ISBN 978-1-55017-726-8 (ebook)

I'd like to dedicate this book to my wife of forty-nine years, Yvonne.
— Bill Proctor

This book is dedicated to Mrs. Ferguson, my Grade 5 teacher at John Norquay School in Vancouver.
—Yvonne Maximchuk

MAP OF BLACKFISH SOUND

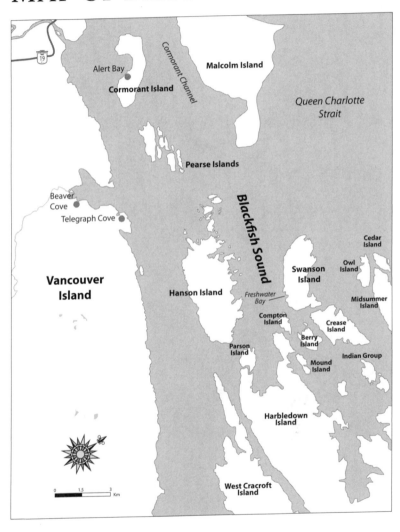

Alert Bay

Cormorant Channel

Malcolm Island

Cormorant Island

Queen Charlotte Strait

Pearse Islands

Beaver Cove

Telegraph Cove

Blackfish Sound

Cedar Island

Owl Island

Swanson Island

Midsummer Island

Hanson Island

Freshwater Bay

Crease Island

Vancouver Island

Compton Island

Berry Island

Parson Island

Indian Group

Mound Island

Harbledown Island

West Cracroft Island

0   1.5   3
Km

CONTENTS

ACKNOWLEDGEMENTS

SOME OF THE STORIES IN THIS BOOK ARE ABOUT THE OLD-time trollers who trolled in Blackfish Sound. These are trollers who sold their fish at our fish camp in Freshwater Bay and I would like to dedicate this book to some of these men, who taught me a lot of what I know today. Back when I started to fish, most of the fishermen were very tight with information. The ones named here took the time to teach me and I will be forever grateful to them.

A special thanks to John Kallas for teaching me how to read the tides, and how to catch the big springs that lurk along the kelp beds; and to Gus Erickson, who gave me some of the coho spoons that he made and also showed me how to make them; and to Scotty Farquharson, who taught me a lot about catching the big springs in Knight Inlet.

I have been asked many times who the most influential people in my life were. First I would have to say my mother, Jae Proctor, who always taught me right from wrong, and who was always there to help me out and give me encouragement. Thanks Mom. Then I would say my father-in-law, Hank Roth, who taught me a lot about logging and how to hook up rigging and to boom logs. After that would be Mel Belveal, who taught me a lot about trapping, hunting and hand logging. Mel was an expert hand logger and unsurpassed as a hunter and a crack shot. Bernard Crowell taught me how to fish off the west coast and out on the banks, and he also taught me not to be afraid of the unknown.

My wife, Yvonne, always gave me support and help no matter what my plans were. And without the help of Yvonne Maximchuk,

I would never have been able to write a book. All these people had a hand in me being able to pass on the stories.

—Bill Proctor

MY GRADE 5 TEACHER, MRS. FERGUSON, TAUGHT ME THAT FIND-ing just the right word is a worthwhile ambition and that sharing words brings knowledge into the lives of others, and pleasure, too. Thank you Billy, so much, for sharing your stories with me, and the years of your generous and educational friendship, out of which grew this beautiful collaboration.

And thanks to you, too, my dear husband, Albert, for always supporting my adventures and ambitions.

—Yvonne Maximchuk

INTRODUCTION

Blackfish Sound: Fishing Beyond Compare

THIS BOOK IS A BIT OF THE HISTORY OF BLACKFISH SOUND, A body of water that lies almost east–west, with Vancouver Island to the south and Knight Inlet to the north. The sound is fed by the waters of Queen Charlotte Strait to the west and the tides are controlled by the mighty Seymour Narrows to the east.

Blackfish Sound is in Fishery Management Area 12. At one time Area 12 was the top producer of salmon on this coast, the reason being that so many runs of salmon passed through the sound to

From the 1966 Cover of Western Fisheries *magazine showing* Storm Prince, Miss Janine *and* Bonnie B.

My dad's boat Helga Hermann *in Leroy Bay, Smith Sound 1929. It is typical of the gillnet boats of that era.* PHOTO BY JAE PROCTOR

get to their spawning grounds. Runs like the big Columbia River spring salmon run used to pass through the sound in vast numbers, and the big runs of white springs going to Toba Inlet and Bute Inlet, as well as a lot of the Knight Inlet springs, and the immense runs that went all the way to the Fraser River.

Blackfish Sound was a very famous troll area; it is shaped like the bottom end of a funnel with strong tides that force the salmon to school up in the back eddies—this is what makes for good fishing. This is the place where a lot of young fishers got their start. A man could buy a small boat and fish there a few seasons, then get a bigger boat and head west. Jack Reinhard came to Freshwater Bay in 1956 in *Grey Hound* with a two-cylinder Easthope engine in it. He was a bit older than me and had just begun fishing. His next boat was *Dran*, then *Miss Janine* and finally the last boat he had in the '80s, as a highliner, was *Island Star III*. Another man I knew about my age was Lorn McKinnell. He had a boat named *Dana*, then he got the *Real McCoy* and his last boat was *Sundance II*, which is still fishing.

It was also where a lot of old-timers liked to troll and they called it "the old man's home."

I have no idea when the first salmon were caught in Blackfish Sound but I would guess about 8,000 years ago. It would have been a Native in a dugout canoe, with a bone hook on a line of twisted cedar or a spear. I can just see a man in a canoe, floating by a big kelp patch, peering over the side, watching for a salmon to swim by so he could spear it. The oldest troller I ever talked to, Ben Bachus, started there in 1919. In this book I will tell about some of these fishermen, and how I learned to fish, read the tides and watch for signs of salmon, as well as the tides of Blackfish Sound.

A BIT ABOUT ME

I WAS BORN AT PORT NEVILLE ON OCTOBER 13, 1934, IN A SMALL cabin in the bush across from the Port Neville Store. A lady named Mrs. Fife was a midwife and she delivered me into this world. A month later Mom and Dad moved to Freshwater Bay on Swanson Island, so that was my home for the next twenty-one years. I had an older sister named Patricia but she died when I was five years old and I don't remember much about her. So I was alone with no other kids around. To amuse myself I took to exploring around the beach in front of our house. I liked it when the tide was real low because I could look at all the creatures on the low tide beach that cannot be seen when the tide is high.

Back then there were no good books on sea life like we have today, so over time I made up names for some of the plants and creatures I saw. I named sea anemones, sea flowers and sea urchins I called sea eggs. The little fish that lived under rocks I called eels and all kelp was simply seaweed.

One day Mom, Jae Proctor, took me on a walk to what she called "the next bay," where I discovered a little tide pool. I was so excited I called Mom to come and see what I'd found. I loved that little tide pool and was after Mom every day to go for another walk to the next bay, but Mom was too busy to go very often. It was a long time before she would let me go by myself. I remember the first day I was allowed to go to "my pool" as I called it. I was seven years old. After that I spent a lot of time watching all the little critters that made their home in the small tide pool. I named all of the little fish that lived in the pool either bullheads

Here I am at five years old in my "going to town" sweater and pressed pants, by mom's garden at Freshwater Bay. PHOTO BY JAE PROCTOR

or sculpins; limpets were china hats, chitons were Indian prunes, all snails were periwinkles and shore crabs were just little crabs.

I learned a lot about the interactions of all the life in the pool. The limpets and chitons were grazers and they lived on the algae growing on the rock surface. This helped to keep the pool rock clean. The sculpins and rock crabs were scavengers and cleaned up anything that died or got washed into the pool.

In the 1940s you never heard the words "habitat" or "environment"; it was just their home. I still go to that pool every year, whenever I am in the area, as I have many fond memories of days gone by, sitting by my little pool. It is the same now as it was when I found it seventy-five years ago; nothing has changed.

In 1946 I bought my first book on fish. I saw it advertised in a fishing magazine and ordered it from the Biological Station in Nanaimo. The package arrived COD at the post office in Alert Bay and I paid for it with money I made fishing spring salmon from my rowboat. The book was called *Fishes of the Pacific Coast of Canada* and remains the best book on fish that I have found. I still refer to it for details about some species. When I got the book I took it with me to my little pool and when I'd find a fish I'd find the name of it in the book. There was a small bay close by that had a lot of crab grass on the bottom. I learned it was called eel grass but I called it crab grass because that was where the big crabs lived. I would take my mom's strainer with me and a bucket, and look for little fish. Over time I identified twenty-two species that called that bay home.

Round about that time there were two missionaries who came once a month to visit Mom. They'd paddle over in a dugout canoe and Mom always told me to go down and help them out of the canoe. So I would and one would always say, "How is the heathen today?" This was because I was not going to school. They were always trying to get Mom to send me to boarding school.

Finally they reported me to Welfare.

Then the government boat called *Sheila* started coming around. I took to hiding in the bush when I saw them coming, so I ended up spending a lot of time in the bush. It really bothered me to think that these people wanted to take me away and leave my mother there alone.

As I was spending a lot of time in the bush, I got to know all the different species of trees and plants that grew on our land. In 1948 a salesman came in selling books, so I bought a ten-volume set of *The Book of Knowledge*, which I still have and I still use.

So instead of going to school I was learning about the things around me. Now, when people come to my museum, some ask me, "How often do you go out in the real world?"

I say, "I think this *is* the real world."

CHAPTER ONE

A NATURAL HISTORY OF BLACKFISH SOUND

Tide Rips and Back Eddies: An Illustration

TIDE RIPS CAN FORM IN A NUMBER OF WAYS. WHAT CAUSES A rip is two tides meeting—for instance if a tide running north meets a tide running south this creates a rip. A rip can also form when there is deep water by the shore and then a shallow bank, reef or point. As the running tide hits the shallow spot or reef, the water boils up and runs faster, and this makes for a rip.

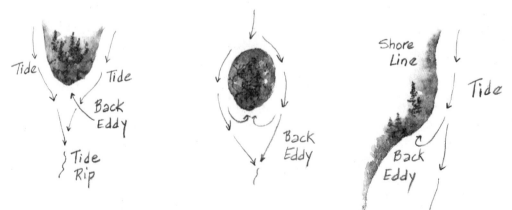

Where tides meet, they will form a Rip

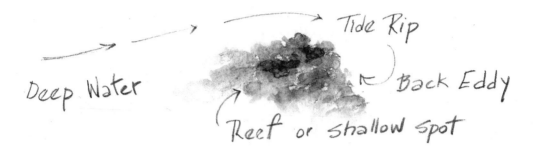

Weather in Blackfish Sound

THE STRONG TIDES AND OPEN WATER OF QUEEN CHARLOTTE Strait can cause some very nasty, confused sea conditions where it narrows into Blackfish Sound.

When there is a big ebb tide flowing out of Weynton Pass and a northeast gale out of Knight Inlet, these conditions produce some real bad tide rips off of Donegal Head on Malcolm Island. This is a bad spot for small boats at this point. It is best to stay on the south side of Stubbs Island and head up toward Freshwater Bay if you are going out to the mainland inlets of the Broughton Archipelago. By doing this you can miss a lot of the rough stuff.

The other bad spot is off the mouth of Knight Inlet. A big ebb tide flowing out of Knight Inlet meeting a westerly gale coming down Queen Charlotte Strait will make for some very big seas. Again it is best to head for Freshwater Bay and go around the back way. It's a bit longer but a lot calmer heading into the Broughton. If you are coming out and heading for, say, Port McNeill, it's best to take the same route if it's blowing westerly, and when you get to Freshwater Bay head across to Hanson Island as it is always calmer there.

When coming home from Port McNeill and a strong westerly wind is blowing and there's an ebb tide off Flower Island, I come down past Alert Bay and down the strait and go through "the blowhole," which is between Hanson and Plumper Islands. Then I run along the shore of Hanson Island and across Blackfish Sound to Whitebeach Pass. These are good ways to avoid the rough spots if you are in a small boat.

I have been in some pretty extreme conditions in Blackfish Sound. One day I was on my way home after dropping the high school kids off. I had to drop them off at Mitchell Bay instead of going all the way to Port McNeill as it was blowing a gale of southeast. I was in my 37-foot fishing boat *Twilight Rock*. When I got near Stubbs Island the wind increased to 85 knots on my wind gauge so I went and hove to behind Stubbs Island and waited for a lull. I could not see across Blackfish for the spray. After an hour or so the wind eased a bit so I idled across Weynton Pass with lots of spray flying and went through the blowhole.

When Mom and I lived at Freshwater Bay we'd go to Alert Bay for supplies and the mail. In 1951, the coldest winter I had ever seen before (or since) brought four feet of snow and the temperature went down to minus six degrees Fahrenheit. It blew northerly gales for sixteen days without let-up. That year there was 31 feet of snow on the flats in the head of Knight Inlet and sustained winds of 100 miles an hour. The deer and mountain goats got trapped on the tidal flats and when the tide rose they could not get through the snowbank to safety and so many were drowned.

In August of 1976 it blew northwest gales for twelve days non-stop. In the morning the wind would be down to 30 knots and back up to 40 in the afternoon. We fished every day and it was *good* fishing. Fish always bite best when it's blowing a westerly. I think they like to come up and play in the aerated waters. Our faces were so windburnt we all looked like tomatoes.

The other extreme I have seen was fourteen days straight of fog, with no breaks; but Blackfish Sound is noted for being a very foggy place.

The sound, however, with all its moods, is a very beautiful place to be on a nice calm day with a clear sky and a beautiful sunset. On days like these you kind of forget the bad days.

Oatmeal in the Spoon Bucket: My Early Days Fishing

WHEN I STARTED COMMERCIAL FISHING AS A TROLLER IN 1943 in Blackfish Sound most of the boats were small and a lot of them were old, much like their owners; but when you are nine years old everyone over forty seems real old. All the trollers who worked Blackfish Sound were known as "day boats," meaning they had to deliver their catch every day as none of the boats were rigged to pack ice and no one had ice to sell anyway. It was not until the 1950s that we started to see an ice packer once in a while.

Fishing would start sometime in July, but August and September were the best months. Fishing would close around October 10. Most of the trollers would fish "bluebacks," young coho, right down in the Gulf of Georgia from opening day on June 15, before heading up to Blackfish. At this time everyone fished for coho and springs only. No one even kept pinks, and sockeye and chum did not bite. There were very few sockeye then. It was not until the late 1950s that the sockeye runs began to rebuild after being almost completely fished out.

Most of the fishermen back then fished alone but the odd one did have his wife on board. These were few because the boats were so small with a very cramped living space. They were known as "bucket boats" because they had no head (toilet). The cabin on these boats consisted of a narrow bunk beside a small table that folded up out of the way. There was a tiny wood stove for heat and a single-burner kerosene Primus stove or a folding Coleman gas stove (like the camp stoves of today) for cooking. Wood for the heater was always a problem. It had to be dry and cut very small because the stove's firebox could only take about seven-inch-long sticks. Many fishermen would burn fir bark for its long-lasting quality. The fishermen spent a lot of time building up piles of the needed firewood on the shore so it would be easy to get at. Some serious fights came about due to one man filching from another man's pile of sticks.

The water supply was, at best, a five-gallon can but most men had only a one-gallon jug, which would be filled each night. Some of the boats and owners were real dirty. Some wore the same clothes for the whole fishing season. They fished in them and slept in them and I knew a few who never once took their clothes off.

The fishing boats were mostly 28- to 30-foot-long double-enders, about seven to eight feet wide, powered by one-cylinder gas engines. The anchor was pulled by hand. The small cabins often leaked when it rained. Many had a little trough around the inside of the cabin wall to keep the water off the bunk. The steering was a system of chains to a tiller in the cockpit. Some boats had a steering wheel at the back of the cabin while some had a pilot- or wheelhouse, but many were just a single cabin with a low door and a sliding hatch to get in and out of. Other boats had a small wooden boxlike shelter to stand in to steer. This was called a "doghouse" and some would slide fore and aft. The fisherman had no phone, no sounder, just a chart and a compass. This was enough though as they pulled the gear by hand, which meant they fished shallow, in close to the shore and the big kelp beds. Most fishermen would just fish early in the morning, then they would anchor until slack tide, then fish the flood, and finally go in to sell the catch. Most would tie up for the night but the highliner would go out for the evening bite.

Many of the boats leaked badly so they had to be pumped out often. This was done with a homemade pump. Some pumps were made of all wood while others were made with four-inch steel pipe; both types worked well and were installed in position on the boat. When I was a boy some of the fishermen liked me to pump their boats and I would go on a boat and pump it out as a favour to them. If the boat leaked like a sieve it could take me fifteen or twenty minutes. Other fishermen would get mad if I went to pump their boats because they did not want people to know their boats leaked. They always pumped them out while out fishing or on their way in, so no one would see them. Once I went on a man's boat and started pumping. It was a steel pump which was real noisy and it woke him up. He came out of the cabin mad as hell and sent me on my way.

Fishing gear was an important topic. Most lures back then were made of brass or golden bronze and the main thing was to keep them shiny at all times. There were no aluminum spoon buckets or Hydrotone in those days so every man had his own idea of how to keep the spoons bright. The main thing was to keep them wet and in the dark; the sun must not shine on them. Some men used a wooden keg to store the spoons. Some used an old battery box with all the insides removed. Some used just any old can, and to these various containers they would add some concoction of their own idea of what was the best brew to keep the spoons shiny bright.

The idea was to make the brew dark so some put their coffee grounds in, some put their tea leaves in, some put soap in and some used hemlock bark. Some swore by alder leaves but the worst by far was oatmeal. Oh God, it used to stink! Oatmeal would ferment and you could smell any boat a long ways off that had oatmeal in the spoon bucket. In 1948 about twenty of us got together and got several aluminum spoon buckets made at a foundry in North Vancouver.

Many of these men were real loners and never mixed with other fishermen. They fished alone all day, came in, sold the catch, got some gas and food and would go and anchor in some bay all alone.

The fisherman's life was suited to the solitary man.

My mom was mostly the only woman around. She'd be busy all day long at our fish camp, Proctor's Fish Camp. She was known as a "cash buyer," meaning she paid each fisherman with cash when he came in with fish. The Anglo-British Columbia Packing Company (owned by Henry Bell-Irving) gave her the cash so each night she had to add up all the fish slips, which could be as many as sixty in a day. Anyone who was counting fish was known as the "tallyman." Her "tally," as she called it, had to "jibe" with the money paid out and the money left on hand. I heard her use these two words many times a day as I was growing up. She had to have the tally ready for

My mom's money box which she packed up and down the dock hundreds of times paying the fishermen cash as she went. PHOTO BY YVONNE MAXIMCHUK

the packer to take with him to the cannery with the fish. He usually showed up around nine o'clock in the morning.

While Mom was adding up the tallies it was my job to look after the store. Most of the fishermen who sold to Mom would stock up at our little store. They mostly were alone on their boats and didn't really eat too well because their food all came in a can. I remember some of the hot items in canned goods we had on the shelves. There was Chuck Wagon dinner, Irish stew, meatballs and gravy, pork and beans, which had to be Heinz. We sold a lot of King Oscar sardines and corned beef, or bully beef as they called it. We also had a lot of bread, pilot bread and hardtack, Empress brand strawberry jam in four-pound tins and Nabob coffee. The fishermen liked the canned foods as they could just open a can, heat it up and eat right out of the can, so no plate to wash. Breakfast would be Shredded Wheat.

Most of the men smoked and Ogden's Fine Cut was the favourite cigarette tobacco. Other favourites were Pickobac Pipe Tobacco and Big Ben Chewing Tobacco and snuff, and rolling papers were ZigZag White and Chanticleer.

Most nights there'd be ten or twelve guys in the store, just sitting around b.s.ing. Some would be playing darts. The topic was always fish. The fish they caught and the fish that got away. I would just sit and listen and give out what everyone wanted. By nine o'clock everyone would have trailed back to their own boat.

Salmon of Blackfish Sound

BEFORE THE 1970S, THE FIRST SALMON OF THE YEAR THAT CAME by Freshwater Bay were bluebacks, young coho about two pounds each with deep blue backs and bright red flesh. These fish were very good eating and we used to can a few as we never caught sockeye in those days. The bluebacks would start to show in mid-April and then they would arrive by the thousands. They came from down in the Gulf of Georgia on their way out to sea.

About June 15, red spring salmon began to show up on their way south to their natal rivers. These fish would be about 14 to 18 pounds each and were quite unique. They were short fish with real thick belly flaps, more than an inch thick and real fat. Their heads were short and round and black. The old-timers told me they were Columbia River springs. I think they had a long way to go up some rocky river, judging from the fatness and the thickness of the belly, which may have been to protect them from a rocky bottom.

The next salmon to show were big white springs. These would show up about July 1 and the run would peak about July 20. They were big strong fish, long and slender and built for speed. When I got my first troller, *Aye-Aye*, I used to love to fish for these salmon. The most I ever caught in one day, July 10, 1966, was twenty-three, with a 28-pound average. On the same day Andy Stadnyk, on the seine boat *Miss Andrea*, had over six hundred in Parson Bay. There were other seine boats in the bay, all fishing springs.

Andy was high boat for three years for the BC Packers plant in Alert Bay. He never left Parson Bay. These big white springs were headed for Knight Inlet, Bute Inlet and Toba Inlet. They spawned in the big glacier rivers at the heads of all the inlets. They were long and slender and powerful in order to buck the rapids and go through narrow canyons.

Mainland pink salmon arrived next. They would show in vast numbers by mid-July and keep coming until early August. Mainland pinks generally come in large numbers on even-numbered years.

On odd-numbered years Fraser River pinks would start to show around the first week in August, and at the same time the Fraser River sockeye would come through. In the last week of August

Blackfish Sound-caught spring salmon, plus one bluish sockeye which I ate for dinner. PHOTO BY BILL PROCTOR

the big coho started to show, heading for hundreds of different streams down the coast, and would go all through September. By mid-September the chums began to arrive and their numbers built until the end of October. Qualicum chums came in last, along with the Nimpkish chums.

The life of the fisherman and the economy of the area around Alert Bay were governed entirely by the repetition and reliable return of these runs of salmon. It shook us up pretty good when they didn't come through according to plan.

Tides of Blackfish Sound

THE DATE IS JULY 20, 1951. THE PLACE IS FLOWER ISLAND IN Blackfish Sound. This is the day the seine boats were waiting for because it is the time of year for sockeye and spring fishing in Blackfish Sound and adjacent waters.

Blackfish Sound is a very unique body of water. One of the reasons for this is all the currents are controlled by the currents flowing through the mighty Seymour Narrows, which stretch roughly 100 miles to the east. It is quite phenomenal that a narrows so many miles away could have an influence on such a large body of water.

On this day in 1951, there are two seiners anchored at Flower Island waiting for the flood tide, at which time they can make a set. They still have about two hours to wait so the crew is playing a game of poker to pass the time. As the time nears when they can make the set the captain climbs up to the bridge to look around while the crew pulls the anchor. The captain then steers the boat close to the shore and looks at the kelp to see which way the kelp is being pulled by the tide.

Because the current at Flower Island is controlled by Seymour Narrows the current won't change direction until around three hours after high or low tide on the shore. What this means is the tide is rising on the shore but the current is still ebbing west. Alert Bay tide tables tell you when the tide will be high or low on the shore. If the Alert Bay tide table says the tide will be low at 10 a.m. for instance, the current won't start to flood east at Flower Island until 1 p.m. or approximately three hours after low tide on the shore.

When the current is ebbing in Blackfish Sound it flows west through Blackney Pass and along past Flower Island and on up along the shore of Swanson Island to Bold Head. At this point the ebb veers more to the north toward Holford Island where it also meets up with the ebb tide from Knight Inlet and Retreat Pass.

There are many other factors taking place where Blackfish Sound meets Queen Charlotte Strait. The current in the strait changes more or less right at high or low tide on the shore.

So here we have a three-hour differential. The current is flooding east down the strait but it is meeting the ebb out of Blackfish Sound at Bold Head. The flood from the strait is also flowing into Knight Inlet and Retreat Pass. As the flood from the strait gets stronger, it starts to push the ebb at Bold Head over toward Hanson Island and down along the shore of Swanson Island to Flower Island. This is what the captain has been waiting for. He can see the flood moving down the shore so he is all set to let the net go when the tide is just right.

And when it is, he hollers, "Let 'er go." He puts the boat full speed ahead as the skiff man ties the end of the net to a tree on a rock, like he has done so many times before.

At the same time all this is taking place, the current from Queen Charlotte Strait is flooding down along the shore of Malcolm Island, from Lizard Point toward Donegal Head, and it meets the ebb flowing north out of Weynton Pass. Where these currents meet are known as tide rips or tide lines. When the salmon are migrating down the strait on the flood tide and they meet the ebb from Weynton Pass, this tends to push them north toward the White Rocks, and then they meet the flood off Bold Head and they get pushed east down along the shore of Swanson Island, then on down to Flower.

Big boils and whirlpools and glossy spots show the power of the tidal push in Blackfish Sound. PHOTO BY YVONNE MAXIMCHUK

At the same time as the crew on the seine boat were playing poker, just a mile or so west in a small bay the trollers named Breakfast Bay, on Swanson Island, two other trollers were anchored, waiting for the current to turn to flood. They would sit on deck and watch the current and as soon as it would start to flow east along the shore, they would pull their anchors and go set their gear.

Though the current is still ebbing west offshore, it is starting to flood east along the shore. This is what is known as a back eddy. The trollers would set their gear one and a half hours before the captain let his net go at Flower Island, so the trollers have a chance to catch some fish in the back eddy before the flood pushes them down to Flower Island for the seiner.

The seiners can only make one set each at Flower Island because by the time they're done, the current is flowing too strong for them to set. They will go and anchor up at Bold Head and wait for the current to ebb out of Knight Inlet.

The trollers will troll down to Flower Island and fish out the flood there, and then at high slack or just as the flood is turning to ebb they will troll back up toward Breakfast Bay and troll there on the first of the ebb. Once the ebb gets flowing too strong, they will go and anchor and wait for the tide or go out for an evening bite.

As the tide was flooding east in Queen Charlotte Strait and into Retreat Pass and Knight Inlet, some fish got pushed along with the current into these places. Some were going up Knight but most were going down Johnstone Strait to the Fraser River. The seine boats are waiting for these fish to back out of Knight Inlet on the first little push of the ebb, so the crew is playing poker again. The end of the net is already tied to shore, the anchor is up, and the captain is on the bridge watching the kelp. As soon as the long bull kelp pops up, which has been pulled under with the current, he hollers again, "Let 'er go."

This was always a very productive set; I've seen seiners load the boat up in this one set. I've seen John Ferry, one of the highline seine captains from Alert Bay, get a deck load in one set on *Silver Bear* more than once. John would wait all day just to get this one set.

WHEN THE EBB STARTS TO FLOW OUT OF KNIGHT INLET IT turns south and meets the flood in Blackfish Sound. It pushes toward Hanson Island and the fish get pushed with it. Many will go through Blackney Pass but some won't make it that far before the current in Blackfish turns to ebb.

When the current turns to ebb out of Blackney Pass it pushes the fish along the shore of Hanson Island toward Double Bay and here they mill around and wait for the next flood to push them on their way down Johnstone Strait.

When the current starts to ebb out of Weynton Pass it flows north toward the White Rocks and there it turns and heads west toward Penfold Island. It also meets the ebb from Knight Inlet and Retreat Pass. This forms a strong tide rip and is a real good place to fish.

Trollers would go and wait for the first of the ebb to come by Stubbs Island and get in the rip, and as the ebb gained velocity it pushed the troller backwards toward the White Rocks. When the ebb is at full flow, the rip will not be a straight line; there will be little holes along the way like little bays in a shoreline. The current will be flowing in circles in these little bays. And this is where fish tend to lie.

The bunt is full of salmon, coming over the roller on this First Nations seine boat in Blackfish Sound. PHOTO BY BILL PROCTOR

If the fish back out of Knight Inlet or Blackfish Sound, they will be on the east side of the rip, but if they are in the current from Weynton Pass they will be on the west side of the rip.

Salmon bite best trolling west or northwest, so some trollers would troll northwest till they were almost out to Penfold Island and then they would pick up their gear and run back east and set their gear and troll northwest again. I never did this because I discovered if I got a school of fish following the gear and I slowed down and turned around fast to get right back into the tide rip, I could keep the school following the gear all the way back to Bold Head. And that is where I wanted to be when the first of the flood started to push into Blackfish Sound.

The tides of Blackfish Sound are a complicated subject and it's taken me forty years to figure it out.

Freshwater Bay

SITUATED NEAR TINY FLOWER ISLAND ON THE SOUTH SHORE of Swanson Island, Freshwater Bay was not a good harbour. The wind would howl into it from the southeast and from the west, and the south wind was the worst. It was known locally as the Nimpkish Wind. It was a tough place to hold floats with both the wind and tide and a long drying beach working against us. We had 400 feet of walkway floats but only 150 feet of them floated all the time; the rest went dry at low tide. We had a big rock anchor at the end of the floats and twelve boomsticks across the bay to hold the floats in place. There were two 30-foot gaps, one on each side of the floats, so boats could get in to tie up.

This is from inside the bay looking across to the other side, showing the entry gap to the right of the scow that ABC (Anglo British Columbia) gave us for fish buying. Left to right are the fuel tank, ice house (we iced fish on weekends) and the outhouse. The scow had large posts for boats to tie to. Ralph's boat is the farthest left. PHOTO BY RALPH SHEMMING

The boomsticks would only last about four years and the boom chains about the same. The reason for this was because the shipworms (teredos) were so bad, they ate up the boomsticks in no time, and the constant movement of the tide and swells wore out the boom chains.

Mom and I had a tough time keeping things in shape after my dad drowned. I was too small to bore the holes in the boomsticks but I could pick one up that was floating by and tow it in with my rowboat. There were a lot of logs floating around back then and it was a real plus to pick up a stick that was bored. But most of the time they were not bored so we would wrap the chain around the end of the log and pound in a staple or two to keep the chain from slipping off. My dad had a big stash of chains because he had been logging. The boat entry gap had ten chains strung across it and the weight of the chains kept the gap deep so the boats could pass over without hitting the chains. I remember one day when I was about fourteen, it was blowing a gale of southeast and a boomstick let go because the chain had pulled out of the hole. Ollie Tiegen on *Beverly* was anchored out (old Ollie always anchored out because he was so fussy he would never let anyone walk across the deck of his boat), and the sticks were looking to wrap around his boat. He was standing on the bow cussing like mad and said if the sticks hit his boat he would shoot me. I got hold of them, using the little outboard boat I had then, towed them back into line and tied them up with a long rope.

Every five years the eyebolt attaching the whole works to the shore had to be replaced because it would rust off. This meant drilling a new hole in the rock. We did this with a rock drill and a 10-pound hammer. One person had to hold the drill while the other hit the drill with the hammer. The one holding the drill had to turn it between swings of the hammer. We could only work at low tide so it would take about four days to drill a hole 10 inches deep. When the hole was done we built a fire to dry the hole out before we sealed the bolt in. If it wasn't completely dry when we poured in the babbitt (a soft white alloy of copper, tin and antimony), it would all spit and bubble out.

A Forgotten Era in Kingcome Inlet

DURING AUGUST OF 1945 THERE WERE ABOUT TWENTY TROLL-ers fishing in Kingcome Inlet, mostly old-timers who had fished Kingcome for over twenty years. They fished mainly coho and the odd chinook. Most years there were a fair number of coho and catches would average about twenty to thirty a day.

August started out like any other year, but around the 10th the trollers down at Sullivan Bay began to get big catches, up to 100 coho a day. Catches like this were unheard of. Soon everyone was catching lots of coho as the run moved into Kingcome. Most of the fleet figured it was just a school that would move through fast. Ten days passed and the trollers down at Sullivan Bay were still catching up to 100 coho a day. The old-timers had never seen anything like it. The troll camp at Sullivan was plugged with fish every night and it was the same at the Simoom troll camp.

The coho kept coming and there were still good catches right up to September 20. It was the largest run of coho anyone had ever seen. No one knew why there were so many because the run in 1942 was just average and as it turned out, 1948 was a poor year.

So where did all the coho come from in 1945, since they are a three-year-old fish? They must have had excellent spawning conditions in 1942 and very good ocean survival, but why was there not a good run in 1948, with so many spawners on the spawning grounds? A lot of people think there were too many fish on the spawning ground. I think this could be right because I have seen this happen in other streams, like Viner River and Bond Sound.

Anyway, whatever it was that caused the run, it was the talk of the fleet for years after. It was just one of Nature's ways of showing us what can happen if conditions are just right. In the next decade, 1957 was another year way above average in Kingcome, but not like the 1945 run. I fished in Kingcome in 1957 and it was common to have 100 big coho a day.

There were thirty to forty trollers in Kingcome that year. The run in 1957 did not last; two weeks and it was all over. I think the reason for some of the big catches was the gear: it was more efficient than in 1945 and trollers were no longer pulling in their catches by hand, as they had power gurdies.

In truth, 1957 was the last good run of coho in Kingcome. In 1968 we saw a small run with six trollers fishing, but that was the last year of commercial trolling for coho in Kingcome Inlet.

The following chart shows the historic runs of salmon to the Kingcome River system, which includes its tributaries: Clear River, Magson Creek, Wild Water Creek, Atlatzi River, Sequilla River and Lahlah Creek.

	HISTORIC RUNS	1953 TO 1973	TODAY
Sockeye	500–600	20–30	unknown
Chinook	25,000–30,000	1,000–1,500	350
Coho	30,000–40,000	5,000–7,000	1,000–1,500
Chum	15,000–20,000	4,000–6,000	500
Pink	one million	avg. 10,000–12,000	600–1,400

Gravel removal for road building has occurred since the early 1900s and continued into the late 1980s. In 1983 the Department of Fisheries and Oceans compiled a gravel removal plan with Whonnock Industries to be activated from 1983 to 1991.

Why would DFO approve a gravel removal plan for what was the best salmon-producing river in the area? It is well known that when gravel is removed from a riverbed, it begins to erode away and the salmon eggs get washed down the river. It takes many years for the gravel to stabilize and become a healthy spawning bed again.

Remember the Lingcod Fishermen?

IN THE 1940S AND '50S THERE WERE FIVE BOATS FISHING A DIF-ferent catch out of Freshwater Bay. They were after lingcod and would come up from the Gulf of Georgia in March when the season opened. There was Walter Redford's *Seacrest*, Percy Strickland had *Kitty S*, *Souvenir* was owned by Robert Bell, there was Murray Taylor's *Essie T* and Harry Pavey had BH.

Cod boats, as they were called, were substantially different from salmon-fishing boats. They had a wheelhouse and small cabin forward along with the engine. There was a cabin on the stern too, which was the living quarters.

The middle of the boat was a live well where the lingcod were kept to keep them alive during the fishing day. The hull of the boat was pierced with holes to let the water in so the bulkheads sealing off the forward and stern parts of the boat had to be really watertight. The holes in the live well were four inches long and one inch wide.

Big live herring were used for bait so each boat carried a small seine net to catch the herring with. These were also kept alive in the boat's live well. The gear consisted of a single-spool gurdy and a 40-pound cannonball. There was a spreader bar which was about five feet long made of three-eighths steel rod. The cannonball hung in the middle and there was a hook on each end of the spreader bar.

When the boats came in to Freshwater Bay, the fishermen had their live pens with them. Each of them had two pens comprised of five eight-foot-square pieces made of 1 x 4 split cedar slats. One piece was for the bottom, the other four were for the sides, and the five were all lashed together with rope to form the square pen. The top was open and they put rocks in the pen to sink them down

Walter Redford's boat Seacrest, *he has it on a homebuilt grid to copper paint the bottom.* PHOTO COURTESY OF WALTER REDFORD

so two feet were left sticking out. The fellows would tie the pens to our docks and when they came in at night, they'd put the day's catch in the pen. This would keep the cod alive until the fishermen had a whole load. When they did, the cod would all be loaded into the live well on the boat and the fishermen would head for Stewart Island, the closest place they could sell their catch. This was a ten-hour run, and they got paid seven cents a pound when they got there and unloaded. These fishermen stayed fairly independent from the salmon fishers. I don't remember any fishing of this style after about 1958.

Glacier Bay Excursions

I SPENT MANY DAYS IN GLACIER BAY UP KNIGHT INLET. I WENT there first in October 1957, and later, from 1962 to 1978, I would spend two months a year fishing up the inlet for spring salmon. I will never forget the first time I went up there to fish. I arrived late in the day so I decided I would just anchor and try fishing in the morning. But when I got close to where I was going to anchor I spied a man in a small boat, fishing with just a brass spoon on a hand line. He was pulling in one fish after another.

It was just about dark but I put out two lines with two lures on each line and before the lines were down there were fish on. I got eight spring salmon before it got too dark to fish.

The man in the small boat was a logger from a camp right in Glacier Bay, so I went and tied up to their rickety, rotten old float and the man came over to talk. He told me he'd caught five springs.

"Fishing is good," I said.

"Not like it was ten days ago," he replied. "We just tied a line to a pike pole and walked along the float and caught all we wanted." So that was my very memorable introduction to Glacier Bay.

When I went up the inlet in 1963, I would back my boat right up to the glacier on a high tide, to chop ice off it to ice down my catch. A big creek comes down the valley from Mount Kennedy,

The glacier can be seen coming down from Mount Kennedy almost to the shore. This is where I used a sawed off mattock to chop ice off to ice down the fish. PHOTO BY BILL PROCTOR

7,200 feet to its peak. It was nice walking up the creek before they logged up and across it.

One day in late October I decided to go goat hunting. I went up the creek until I came to where it runs out from under the glacier. The creek ran out of an ice cave so I walked right in. The cave was about 60 feet high and about 70 feet wide and the ice was very blue. It was all quite unstable though so I did not go in very far. I backtracked and worked my way up until I was on top of the ice. There was a bit of new snow on the glacier so I walked on for a while and saw lots of deer tracks. Then I came upon a big bear track, a grizzly track. I followed that for a bit and found the track kept going over to a big crack in the ice. The track told me the bear would stop, then walk a bit, then stop again. At one place, the bear laid down right at the edge of the crevasse. I took a look myself and saw it was about 100 feet down to the creek.

The crack was narrow, only a couple feet wide, the ice was about 60 feet thick, a transparent blue, and lying on the bank of the creek 40 feet further on down was a dead mountain goat. It appeared to have come down on a snow slide and I guess the bear caught a whiff of the dead animal coming up the narrow crack in the ice.

Sockeye 1958: The Turning Point

THE YEAR 1958 WAS A TURNING POINT FOR COMMERCIAL TROLL-ers on the BC coast. That was the year we learned how to catch sockeye, and in some ways that was a bad omen for the future. In 1958 the big Adams River run of sockeye came on the inside waters through Blackfish Sound and down Johnstone Strait instead of down the west coast of Vancouver Island. Prior to 1958 trollers caught very few, if any, sockeye. They mainly caught spring salmon and coho and pinks.

At the start of the 1958 season, July 15, there was the usual bunch of boats, mostly old-timers, fishing springs. Fishing was poor in July but started to pick up around the first of August, when a few pinks showed up. Then on August 10 all hell broke loose.

Some boats came in that night with up to four hundred sockeye. It caused a lot of talk among the members of the fleet. The old diehards said it was just a flash in the pan and these boats had just been lucky and had run into a school of sockeye going through. The next night it was the same only more boats had sockeye. The boats that were catching sockeye were not catching coho or springs. This had some of the old diehards baffled and some of them had to finally admit that these guys who were catching the sockeye had some new gear and were fishing differently.

Soon the secret was out. "Abe and Al" flashers were the hot item, and fishing offshore and fishing deep was the new way. Prior to 1958 everyone fished along the beach and amongst the kelp where the big springs and coho liked to lurk. They never fished deeper than 8 to 10 fathoms (48 to 60 feet). In order to catch the sockeye one had to fish below 20 fathoms and on down to 40 fathoms (120 to 240 feet).

Most of the old trollers never had that much line on their gurdies, or cannonballs heavy enough to fish that deep. In 1958, Abe and Al flashers were a new item on the market. Most of us had never heard of them let alone seen them; it was a whole new ball game. All the fishermen wanted Abe and Als so my mom put in an order for four hundred, but she received only one hundred. Since Abe and Als were so new to the market the big gear stores that Mom bought from hadn't stocked very many, in case they didn't sell well.

And so it went. Catches remained high and more boats were showing up. When the sockeye first showed up in Blackfish Sound there were only about fifty boats but in less than a week there were over two hundred. Word had spread fast, which was odd as very few boats had radiophones back then.

By the 20th of August the run was still coming in strong and there were fish jumping everywhere. Boats were coming in loaded every night. It was about this time that problems began to build up. Problems like packers being unable to handle the huge volumes of fish or fish camps (like ours) running out of gas and food, and buying fishing gear became next to impossible.

The packers presented the worst problem as the catch had to be taken to Steveston down on the Fraser River. This made for a lot of running time. Some of the catch was taken to the BC Packers plant at Namu. Seine boats and gillnetters were fishing four days a week and trollers were fishing seven.

In an average year at our camp, which had been at Yokohama Bay since 1956, the packer would tie up all day, and then take the day's catch down to Growler Cove each night to meet the big packer. That August of 1958 the packer had to make two trips a day because our camp could not hold a full day's catch. These packers also ran to Alert Bay to pick up food and freight for our store.

Our packers were *Tsuru*, which was owned by Johnny Demetus, who was known coastwide as "Johnny the Greek," and *Margan*, owned by Fred Seegans. These were small packers. *Tsuru* was 40 feet long with a small cabin on the stern but could pack a pretty fair load. *Margan* was only 36 feet long, unable to pack as much, so most of the trips to Alert Bay were made by old Fred.

As the size of the fleet increased, gas became a big problem. Boats would come from the Double Bay camp and sell their fish to us in order to be able to buy gas. This was a problem because we liked to get their fish but wanted to be able to provide the gas to our steady fishermen. In those days most fishermen were very loyal to the company they fished for. The trollers who fished out of Double Bay wanted to be loyal to the Canadian Fishing Company, and did not really like to come to our camp to sell their catch, and it was the same for the fishermen who sold to us, who were loyal to Mom.

At the peak of the run, which lasted almost a full month, a lot of the boats would have to take time to run to Alert Bay for gas and grub, which meant lost fishing time. Most of the boats were small and did not pack much gas so it meant going to Alert Bay every two or three days. Our gas tank held only 3,000 gallons and the tanker came in to fill it once a week. With a fleet of eighty boats it did not take long to empty the tank, so my mother started to ration the gas. If a man asked for 50 gallons Mom would give him 25 gallons. Because she did this, most boats at our camp were able to keep fishing.

Fishing gear was another big problem. It was such a new trend and it happened so fast that no one was prepared for it. The Abe and Al flashers were hard to get and the ones that did come in were always spoken for. The old type of flashers weaved back and forth in the water, but the Abe and Als were the first spinning flasher.

The reason no one had tried to spin the homemade flashers was because there were no ball-bearing swivels. Without them the leaders would just twist up in no time. Before Abe and Al flashers came along, all the flashers were handmade by the fishermen, although there were fishermen who were willing to pay ten dollars a flasher if they could get them. I know ten dollars may not sound like much now, but considering Abe and Al flashers sold for a dollar fifty each, it was a lot. It was the same with certain lures. The Scott Plastics Flasher Flicker Sockeye Red was the hot lure. They came fifty to a box and the box cost about five dollars. Mom had fishermen offer her ten times that for a box, if she could get them. Abe and Al flashers and Flasher Flickers would revolutionize the trolling industry coastwide.

By the end of August the run was slowing down a bit but there was still good fishing. Some of the fishermen were getting tired and many had sore hands but most had made more money than they had ever dreamed of. Fifty dollars had been considered a good day prior to 1958, but now fishermen were making three to four hundred dollars a day and a high boat might make as much as six hundred dollars. Ellis Mornay on *Kath-Ell* made seven hundred and sixty dollars in one day and his catch made the front page headlines of the *Vancouver Sun*.

One young man, Wayne Bolton, was fishing with his uncle on his troller *Reef Point*. They'd been doing well fishing sockeye but they could never catch any spring salmon. Wayne asked if he could go fishing with me one day when I would be fishing springs. I said yes, so a few days later we went to Cockatrice Bay and we pulled in twenty-one spring salmon, and the two in the photo were the largest at 40 and 42 pounds dressed. He was a happy lad

Wayne Bolton with the two largest springs caught at Cockatrice Bay.

PHOTO COURTESY OF THE BOLTON FAMILY

and in 2014 I received a letter from him with this photo taken on my mother's fish-buying float.

The sockeye run was over by September 15 but that was not the end of the story. A lot of the fishermen went to the bars after they got home and bragged about all the money they made fishing sockeye in Blackfish Sound. There is always the odd person who likes to exaggerate and there is always someone who is willing to listen, and there were plenty of tall tales. During the winter of 1958–59 there was a lot of talk around the Lower Mainland about the fortune that could be made fishing sockeye in Blackfish Sound.

One friend of mine told me about two men who were digging a ditch in front of his house. He was working on his lawn so he overheard them talking about the big money they could make next summer fishing sockeye up in Blackfish. One man said come spring he was going to buy a boat and go fish sockeye up in Blackfish Sound and the other man said when you get there, make sure you fish out of Double Bay camp because the boats that fish out of there make six to seven hundred dollars a day and the boats that fish out of Proctor's camp only make three to four hundred dollars a day. I think this idea came about because of the way the *Vancouver Sun* wrote the story about Double Bay fisherman Ellis Mornay and his big catch.

So it went all winter and come spring any boat that would float was bought and rigged for trolling. Some were just junkers and never left the dock and some were rigged so haywire that when they did get to Blackfish Sound they could not fish.

Another friend of mine had his boat tied to a dock in False Creek where a man was rigging up an old gillnet boat for trolling. My friend was watching and told the man the way he was putting on the gurdies was no good. The man replies, "I know it's haywire but those guys up in Blackfish Sound make six to seven hundred dollars a day so I will have no problem making three or four hundred a day."

It is important to note that that the run of Adams River sockeye in 1958 was sixteen million, the largest run since 1913. They were all four-year-old fish from a run that had been building on each cycle year. Out on the west coast, no one had used flashers, only spoons, so no sockeye were caught. In this remarkable year, the sockeye had come down the inside passages and that, along with the Abe and Al flashers, is what made for the incredible fishing.

So all over the coast, it was like a gold rush, with dozens of men getting ready to go to Blackfish Sound to seek their fortune. Some guys sold their house to buy a boat and a lot of them never did wet a line. The ones that made it to Blackfish Sound in 1959 never caught a sockeye because that year they went down the west coast of Vancouver Island as usual. May 17, 1959, I was out trolling in Blackfish Sound to catch a salmon for supper. As I was trolling along I saw another troller coming, a small, haywire-looking outfit. When it got closer to me, I saw there was a man in the trolling cockpit dressed in rain gear even though it was a beautiful sunny day.

The man steered over to me and hollered, "Where are all the sockeye?"

I hollered back, "You are two and a half months too early and one year too late." Almost every day through June and July many boats came along looking for last year's sockeye. Some of these poor souls must have been dreadfully disillusioned.

To make matters worse in 1959, the whole fishing fleet went on strike July 29 and stayed out until August 10. This was a bad blow for everyone, and especially for all the newcomers. I felt sorry for

1960–Trollers at Yokohama Bay. Note the licence number on foreground boat includes the owners initials. PHOTO BY JAE PROCTOR

them because there was no way they could make a cent, and to tie to the dock for a couple weeks is tough for anyone. When the strike ended there were so many boats the DFO count was three hundred. We were allowed to fish for four days and then DFO closed Blackfish Sound for trolling. This was the first time trolling had ever been closed, but it had to happen because there were so many boats. It was complete chaos. Once you got in amongst the fleet you just had to go along, there was no turning until the fleet turned.

When DFO closed Blackfish Sound, fishing was still open above Port Hardy, so we all went up there to fish. I was fishing at Scarlett Point and doing well, and it was close to the fish camp at God's Pocket. A man named Pete McWilliams ran the camp, gas dock and small store. Pete was a very nice man but

I kept the strike notices from 1959 and hung them in the museum in the fishing section. PHOTO BY YVONNE MAXIMCHUK

he was the no-nonsense type so he was having a little fun with all the greenhorns, teasing them about all the sockeye around and their haywire boats.

Pete had very little dock space to tie up to so the dock was plugged every night. I would go and anchor out but a lot of boats had no anchor. One fellow had a small boat about 26 feet long with a cabin made of shakes and a peaked roof just like a house. There was another small boat with its gurdies and the davits mounted in the centre of the boat instead of at the stern, so the lines went up and over the side of the boat and were sawing into its wooden sides.

I was up at Pete's camp late in September 1959 when one day a man came in. He was a nice young man but his boat was real haywire: about 26 feet long and powered with a motor out of an army jeep. I sat and talked with him and he told me he was from Vancouver and had come up north expecting to make some big money. He had started on the first of June and had fished all the way up to Prince Rupert and back. When he left Vancouver in the spring he had told his mom and dad he was going north to make his fortune fishing sockeye. His dad had helped him buy his boat and now it was the twenty-fifth of September and he had not caught one sockeye. He had caught coho and pinks but no sockeye. He was a real sad young man but he said he had learned a good lesson: not to jump into some project just from hearsay.

There was also a man and wife who came to our camp by the name of J.P. Engleheart and his boat's name was *Clymar*. It was a 36-foot-long cabin cruiser and the cabin went almost to the stern, with just enough room to stand. No cockpit, the gurdies were on the cabin roof, the motor was up in the fo'c'sle and the gurdies were run with shafts and belts from the motor. One can

Annie Tuck, working as a cash buying fish packer; all the packers flew a company flag. PHOTO BY YVONNE MAXIMCHUK

only imagine what the inside of the cabin looked like with shafts, pulleys and bearings dripping grease and oil.

The wheelhouse was well forward with a door on each side of the fo'c'sle, and inside was a big old clawfoot tub. Seeing he had nowhere on the stern to keep the fish, he took them through the cabin and put them into the tub. When he came in at night to deliver, his wife would hand him the fish out of the bathtub and he would toss them out the wheelhouse door. J.P. had another odd trait. When he was out fishing he would climb the mast and sit on the crosstrees. It used to scare the wits out of his wife so I asked him why he did this. He said he was looking for sockeye jumping because he had been told he had to find a jumper before he could catch some.

There was another boat named the *Amerald Queen*, a big old boat 40 feet long. It was all black decks and the hull was tarred and the owner looked like he had been tarred too, because everything he touched was tar. He was a middle-aged man but was a poor-looking soul and his boat was haywire like most of them. He could not catch fish and he came to me one night and asked me to help. He offered me fifty dollars a day if I would go fishing with him to show him how to catch fish. I would have liked to have gone with him but him and his boat were both so dirty I declined, but I did go to work on his gear and I could not believe what he had.

He seemed to have a bit of money so I took him over to Mom's store and got him to buy what he needed. I rigged his gear like mine and told him how deep to fish and to watch where other boats were fishing. I also told him to get the tar and oil and grease off his hands or to wear gloves while he was fishing. Well, he came in the next day with a fair catch and I had a new friend.

So that's the way the season of 1959 went: not many fish and a lot of disillusioned men, but that's what happens at any gold rush.

Fishing Gear Order to Edward Lipsett, 1940s to '50s

4 dozen No. 5 ½ Wonder Spoons brass
2 dozen No. 6 Wonder Spoons brass

3 dozen No. 1 Gibbs Egg Wobblers brass

2 dozen No. 2 Backman Wobblers brass

50 sheets 20-gauge brass Spoon metal 10 sheets
   20-gauge Golden Bronze Spoon metal

20 boxes No. 7-0 Black Mustad Hooks

10 boxes No. 8-0 Mustad Hooks

4 boxes No. 9-0 Mustad Hooks

10 boxes No.6-0 xxx Mustad Hooks

10 boxes No. 8-0 Pacific Brand Mustad Hooks

6 boxes No. 9-0 Pacific Brand Mustad Hooks

4 boxes No. 7-0 Harrison Hooks

4 boxes No. 7-0 DeWitt Hooks

2 gross each No. 9, 10, 11 and 12 Brass Split Rings

1 gross Corkscrew Swivels brass

1 gross Quick Change Swivels brass

2 gross Barrel Swivels brass

12 cans Brasso Spoon Polish

6 cans Bonton Spoon Polish

6 bottles White Way

6 bottles Ioka (these last two items would turn
   brass to silver)

12 spools Donegal Cutty Hunk size 32

12 spools Donegal Cutty Hunk size 36

24 rolls Willlstay Bright Leader Wire No. 8

24 rolls Willlstay Bright Leader Wire No. 9

24 rolls Willlstay Bright Leader Wire No. 10

24 hanks Green Cotton Line size 72

24 hanks Green Cotton Line size 84

24 hanks Green Cotton Line size 96

12 Gaff Hooks

50 feet Rubber Tubing
1 gross Tubing Connectors, plain eyes
1 gross Tubing Connectors, swivel eyes
36 Mainline Swivels
36 Spreader Bars
12 Trolling Springs
24 Trolling Bells

MY DAD WOULD BUY PIG LEAD IN 50-POUND BARS AND MELT it down to two-, three- and five-pound lead weights. He had moulds to make lures, which I still have. The largest mould he used was 10 pounds and he would buy these from Lipsett.

Forty-five Years in the Life of the Native Fisherman, 1930–75

"KLAHOWYA TILLICUM." THIS IS THE WAY THE OLD NATIVE people would greet my parents and me when they came to our store and post office at Freshwater Bay in the late 1930s and '40s. As a boy living there I liked to see the Natives come as they would always tell me stories, they always laughed a lot, and to me, they seemed happy and carefree. The people came from Mammalilaculla (Mimkumlis) on Village Island, New Vancouver (Tzatsisnukomi) on Harbledown Island and Karlukwees (Ka Lugwis) on Turnour Island. Some of the people got their mail from our post office but others picked it up in Alert Bay.

In those days most of the men owned a gillnetter and some had seine boats. Each spring the Native gillnet fishermen would get ready to go to Smith Inlet to fish sockeye. They would head north for the inlet about the end of June. Most of the fishing was done in the mainland inlets and channels. The seiners all had their favourite spots to fish, which were always at the boundary of some river or stream.

Three of the best hot spots were Bond Sound, Thompson Sound and Viner Sound. The boundaries in these inlets were designed for seiners and gillnetters. In Kingcome Inlet, Knight Inlet and Wakeman Sound there was a purse seine limit, and the gillnet area was inside the purse seine limit, closer to the river mouth. Purse seining was allowed in Kingcome up to the mouth of Wakeman Sound and up to Glendale Cove in Knight Inlet. No seining was allowed inside Wakeman Sound but it was a good gillnet fishing area.

After the sockeye fishery in Smith Inlet ended around July 15, the gillnetters would come back to our area and go fish coho salmon in Wakeman Sound or up in the heads of Knight Inlet and Kingcome. The seiners would fish for the vast schools of pink salmon heading for Knight and Kingcome Inlets. It was quite common for them to get a full load in one set. If there was no packer to take their catch they would go to the cannery and unload the fish. The cannery at Charles Creek in Kingcome Inlet operated from 1906 until 1930. My mom and dad lived there for a year before it was shut down and then spent winters there as caretakers until the slide took out the cannery in 1933. The cannery in Glendale Cove in Knight Inlet operated from 1915 until 1950. I don't know when the Bones Bay cannery began operating but it closed down around 1966.

These canneries relied mainly on the pink salmon for the bulk of their production. Some years there were so many pinks the cannery could not keep up and a lot of salmon ended up being dumped overboard.

Each cannery employed about one hundred workers. A lot of these workers were Native or Chinese women, but most of the net men were Japanese. They would work all winter making nets, mending them when torn, and also take care of the boats. The Chinese women dressed the fish and washed them and got them ready to put in the cans. The Native women filled the cans, put the lids on and got the cans ready to place in the retorts (cookers).

By the end of August when the pink run was over, the gillnetters would put on their larger mesh nets and begin fishing for chum salmon. Back then most gillnetters had only two nets, a net for sockeye with five-inch mesh and a coho net with six-inch mesh. Sometimes the net varied a bit in size so a sockeye net might be five and a quarter inches and a coho net might be six and a half inches. All nets were 200 fathoms (1,200 feet) long and sixty meshes deep.

The chum fishing was best from September 1 until mid-October. Besides being canned, a lot of the chums were salted. There were salteries at Freshwater Bay and Alert Bay, and one in Glendale Cove. The canned chum was labelled as "Keta," the Latin name for chum salmon.

Viner Sound and Shoal Harbour were the hot spots for the seiners. The gillnetters fished Kingcome and Wakeman and the head of Knight Inlet. Some of the seiners fished Bond and Thompson Sounds for chum salmon. Very little gillnetting was done in Tribune Channel because there were too many dogfish. Some seining was done around Fife Sound.

At the time, seine boats were much smaller than they are today and not very powerful, so they could not fish where there was much tide or wind. Their nets were shallower than modern nets and had to be pulled by hand. Almost all the gillnetting was done at night because the nets were coarse and the fish could see them in the daylight. Some of the gillnets used were white and with these nets the fishermen could fish the milky waters in the heads of the inlets. The white colour of the sea was due to run-off from the glaciers.

Each of the canneries had net rack floats for the fishermen to work on their gillnets on the weekends. Each float had bluestone (copper sulphate) tanks. All the nets were made of Irish linen and had to be put in bluestone to cut the slime off or the nets would rot. There were net rack floats in Moore Bay, Kingcome Inlet and in Ahnuhati in Knight Inlet.

The seiners would all go to the canneries to do net work. Their nets were made of cotton so were prone to rot. To prevent this some were tarred and some were placed in a tank with "cutch," a dye and net preservative similar to bluestone. This coloured the nets brown and kept them from rotting.

When the pink run was on through July and August, each cannery would have big packers in Moore Bay, Kingcome Inlet and Hoeya Sound in Knight Inlet, and at Kumlah Island and Kwatsi Bay, both in Tribune Channel. These big packers were for the seine fleet. The seine boats always went to the packer to unload the catch. For the gillnetters, the canneries had a lot of small collectors to go around and pick up the catch every morning. When the chum were running in Viner Sound and Shoal Harbour there would be packers anchored at Powell Point and in Echo Bay.

Once the salmon season closed around the fifteenth of November, most of the Natives who had gillnet boats would get ready to go trapping. There were about twenty-five trappers in the area and their trapping season opened on December 1 and ran to the end of February.

The Native people who trapped around the islands would also dig clams but the ones who trapped up the inlets did not have this opportunity, as there were no clams up the inlets due to the fresh water from the glaciers. Clam-digging season began around October 1 and ran until the end of April. BC Packers placed a big scow at Gilford Village (Gwayasdums) to buy clams from all the diggers in the area. They had a big packer to take the clams to Alert Bay to be shipped to Vancouver on the Union Steamships boat.

Some of the Native people worked in the small logging camps in the area and a lot of the older men and women would go to fish halibut in the spring. Fishing with their "handy billy" gear was usually very successful and they would cut the halibut into long strips and hang them on racks to dry in the sun and wind. There were drying racks at Whitebeach Pass, Baronet Pass, Providence Pass and Spiller

Carver Sam Johnson from Gwayasdums (Gilford Village) was one of those who fished with his boat Leda *during the 1950s.* PHOTO BY YVONNE MAXIMCHUK

Pass, with houses to live in at all these sites, as the people might spend up to two months at this work.

In the fall, October and November, there were salmon to smoke and hang to dry. The Native people would go to Viner Sound, Shoal Harbour and Bond Sound to smoke chum salmon. They would take the salmon that were ready to spawn right out of the river because these salmon had no fat left on them, would keep well and would not go rancid.

In the late 1940s and '50s the runs of pink salmon to the inlets were on the decline due to overfishing. At the same time, the runs of sockeye to the Fraser River were increasing. Due to the fact that pink salmon were worth only five cents each and sockeye were netting seven cents a pound there was a lot less fishing in the inlets and much more out in Johnstone Strait and Blackfish Sound. However, a lot of the gillnetters who fished comfortably in the inlets were too small and haywire to go "outside," as it was called. A lot of the Native people quit fishing at this time, but some got themselves a bigger boat and continued.

Some of the small, under-powered seine boats had a tough time trying to fish sockeye because their nets were too shallow and they did not have enough power to work in the strong tides that occur on the outside. This continued all through the '50s and '60s and then into the '70s the price of pink salmon went up to forty cents a pound (in contrast, today the price of pink salmon is about thirty cents a pound). The result was an increase in fishing in the inlets and channels again. By then it was a transformed fishery, with drum seiners and tangle gillnets that could catch more fish in one day than could previously be caught in four days. At the same time, Area 12 had been subdivided into thirty-six sub-areas so there was no more boundary fishing. The last big fishery in the inlets was 1973 and 1974. Since then there has only been the odd small fishery contained to small sub-areas.

When fishing was good there were four hundred people employed in the canneries for about four months of the year. Over six hundred fishermen of all races relied on the fish in the mainland inlets for a major part of their yearly income. This was a very sad time for the Native fishermen of the mainland inlets. After the runs of pinks and chums declined, due to drum seining, tangle gillnets and clear-cut logging of all the fish-bearing watersheds, and the canneries closed down and DFO was forced to close all the mainland inlets to commercial fishing, it became much harder

Most of these boats at the Alert Bay dock in 1957 were owned by First Nations fishermen. PHOTO BY YVONNE PROCTOR

for the indigenous people to make a living here. Now there is no commercial fishing in the inlets, plus no trappers, no hand loggers and no small power-logging outfits where once a guy could always get a job. The only income-earning activity left is clam-digging and there is very little of even that. It had been a great way of life. I know because I shared it. I was fishing just the same on the inside waters close to home, where the familiar runs came in reliably and we could be there to meet them.

Handy Billies

A SHORT LENGTH OF GILLNET UP TO 20 FATHOMS LONG WAS ONE meaning of the words "handy billy." The 20 fathoms could be used alone or added to the real gillnet to lengthen it. All gillnets were 200 fathoms long but if you added the handy billy your net would be 220 fathoms long. These were never used if there was a chance of getting caught by DFO, and DFO was always on the lookout for them.

Some trollers I knew did have a handy billy and I was accused of having one a few times. The reason for this was because I was always the first boat out in the morning and the last one in at night. People imagined I went out early to pick it up and stayed out late to set it.

But the fishermen that I knew had them used to go and fish coho outside Wells Pass and they would come sell the catch to us. A lot of the fish had net marks on them, which troll-caught fish never do. These fishermen would troll all day and then set the handy billy at night in some quiet little bay.

This term was also used for a type of Native halibut fishing gear used in the days when they made halibut hooks from yew wood, steamed in a mould to make the wood soft enough to bend. The handy billy was a string of three floats attached to each other about 20 feet apart. A line was suspended from the first float down to the fishing gear, which consisted of a six-foot spreader bar with two hooks hanging from it. A rock weight, attached with braided cedar line, hung in the centre, about 28 to 30 inches from the spreader bar. Each of the two side hooks hung about 20 inches from the bar so they floated about a foot off the bottom and did not drag. The original wooden halibut float, yew wood spreader bar and braided cedar line went out of use by the time I was fishing; instead a quarter-inch steel rod was used and modern fishing line and floats. The bait was

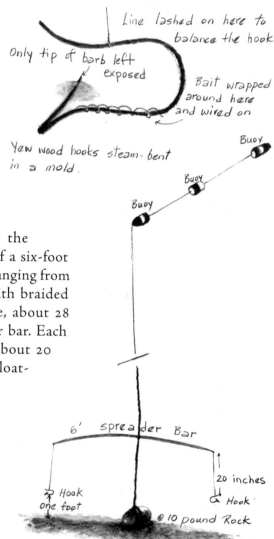

Line lashed on here to balance the hook

Only tip of barb left exposed

Bait wrapped around here and wired on

Yew wood hooks steam-bent in a mold.

Buoy

Buoy

Buoy

6' spreader Bar

20 inches

Hook one foot

Hook

@ 10 pound Rock

wrapped around the halibut hook and wired on, leaving just the tip of the barb exposed.

The buoy would float the spreader bar and when a halibut bit the bait, the first buoy would bob down so the fisherman knew he had one on.

Usually the Native fisherman would have about four of these set out at one time and would sit in his canoe and watch. As soon as he saw a buoy sink he would go and pull it in. Sometimes a big halibut would pull more than one buoy under as it headed for deep water. Because a halibut's mouth opens vertically and not horizontally, no fish but a halibut can get on the hook, although once in a while a big lingcod would swallow the whole hook.

Chinook Language: A Brief Dictionary

IN THE EARLY DAYS BOTH WHITE AND ABORIGINAL PEOPLE spoke Chinook, especially if they did business with each other, like in the fishery or trading store. The language is a mix of Native tongue, some English, Scottish and French, and maybe Chinese mixed in. Because English does not have many of the glottal stops that the Aboriginal tongue does, and the differences people from disparate language backgrounds have in their "sounds library," Chinook evolved into a mishmash language that served for reasonably reliable communications between peoples. The French influence is very obvious in words like thank you (marcie), and pipe (la peep). My dad could speak Chinook really well and the following is a list of words that would cover just about anything a person would need to communicate.

Fish: Pish
Salmon: Sabud
Clams: La-Kootche
Oysters: Klock-Kloch
Bear: Itsoot
Otter: Ninamox
Whale: Quance
Seal: Clikhiyou
Porpoise: Quiceo

Anything good to eat:
   Muck Muck
Oats: La Wane
Venison: Mowitch
Milk: Tootoosh
Cranberries: Cold Oleally
Butter: Tootoosh-Gleece
Potato: Wapito
Flour: Kleeman Sapalel
How Much: Konsick
Rum: Lum
Drunk full of rum: Patlum
Exchange or barter:
   Hooey-Hooey
Tobacco: Kianoose

Chief: Tyee
Old Woman: Lemeyi
Old Man: Oloman
Friend: Six

Dog: Kramox
Mouse: Soulee
Rooster: Le Cock
Birds: Kulla Kulla
Eagle: Yakulla
Duck: Mauk
Hawk: Shamirk
Grouse: Smock-Mock
Owl: Waugh-Waugh

Moccasins: Skin Shoes
Spade: Lapell
Knife: Opsu
Axe: Le-Hash
Nail: Leglow
Rope: Lope
Pants: Seeclicks
Beads: Kamoosak
Cloth: Sil
Ribbons: Lalopa
Petticoat: Keek Wully Coat
Cup: Oskan
Chair: La Chaise
Pipe: La Peep

Understand: Numtux
Thanks: Marcie
Stop talking: Kopet Waw
   Waw

Listen: How
Music: Tin Tin
Heart: Tum Tum
Nothing: Kultus
Plenty: Hi You
Take: Iscum

Today: One One Sun
Snow: Cold-Snass
Rain: Snass
Wind: Toto
Stars: Klaksee
North: Stowbelow
South: Stagwarm
East: Sun Chako
West: Sun Midnight
Winter: Cold Sun
Summer: Warm Sun

One: Ikt
Two: Mox
Three: Klone
Four: Locket
Five: Quinam
Six: Taghum
Seven: Sinamox
Eight: Stotekin
Nine: Quies
Ten: Totilum

Swim: Shetsham
Cook: Capeau
Sleep: Moosum
Capsize: Killipie
Shoot: Pooh
Kill: Mimaloose

Quick: Hyack
Slow: Klawa
Heavy: Till
Red: Pill
Good: Kloshe
Bad: Mesatchy
Strong: Skookum
Large: Hyass
Small: Tenass
Long: Yoolkut

Eleven: Totilum-De-Ikt
Twelve: Totilum-De-Mox
Hundred: Ikt Tokamonak
Thousand: Ihkyass
    Tokamonak

Sockeye 1998

HERE IT IS, 1998, AND WE ARE ALL READY TO GO AND CATCH some sockeye so I pick up Yvonne's daughter Theda Miller and go to Port McNeill to pick up my grandsons, Glen and Derek Hoddinott, and we go to Port Hardy for fuel and grub and a bit of new gear. While I am in the gear store I see a notice from DFO that we need a logbook and we also need an amendment for the fishing licence to permit fishing in Area 11.

Sockeye fishers at work: me, my grandson Glen Hoddinott and Yvonne Maximchuk's daughter Theda Miller. PHOTO BY DEREK HODDINOTT

I go to attend to all the paperwork and send the kids to shop for grub but while I am at the DFO office I find out the opening has been postponed for three days. I run to find the kids and tell them the news and find them with two carts full of groceries. We have to go and put it all back on the shelves, which got us some odd looks from people. I can't say I blame them. We get on the boat and head back to Port McNeill, the boys go home, Theda takes the floatplane back to Echo Bay, and I sit and wait.

I had just put in a new freezer unit and it was not working well so while I'm in McNeill I get it fixed and now it seems to be OK.

July 30 is the big day and the crew returns and we are on the fishing grounds at daylight and we start catching fish right away. We end up with a fair day's catch, lots of small problems but no big deal. I spend most of the day watching the freezer and worrying about whether it will break down. I put fifty fish on trays and the temperature in the hatch rises 12 degrees.

What now? I am thinking. But an hour later the temperature is back down so I feel I know what to expect.

Day two we have a good start but then we have a bad tangle. Two of the pigs (the floats that hold the lines away and back from the boat) decide to get tangled, or mate as I call it, and there are a lot of bad words. We lost a few flashers and lures but that is all part of the game of trolling for sockeye.

I remember when I fished alone years ago I would fish all season without a single tangle, but in those days we fished shallow and only had four lures. Now we fish six lines with sixteen to twenty lures on each line, but it is easy to blame it on the deckhands. And when you have three of them you can really give 'em hell.

Day three we are off to a good start when all hell breaks loose. First we lose a pig line and all the gear on it so I try to turn to pick it up. What with the wind and tide and big swells I miss it on the first pass and in the process the other pig decides to take off and the remaining two pigs mate. We pick up the lost pigs on the second try so now there is just the mess to untangle. We lost a few flashers but are soon back fishing with all six lines.

I'd been thinking that by now, everything that could happen had happened, but I was wrong. Fishing lines break, they jump off the drum, snaps go in the blocks all on their own with no one's help. While all this is going on I am watching the freezer like a hawk and all of a sudden the compressor starts to scream like hell. I yell at the kids to pick up the gear and I phone the freezer man and he is waiting on the dock when we get there.

"Start up the compressor," he says, so I do.

"Slow it down," he says, "it's turning too fast." I slow it down and it seems to be fine but there is a noise that doesn't sound quite right to him. I let the compressor run all night and by morning the hatch temperature is down to −42 degrees.

We head back out to the fishing grounds and all goes well until the bilge alarm goes off. I dive down into the hatch and there's water down there alright, and the pump hose is frozen solid and the hand pump is also frozen.

With the freezer temperature so cold I am really beginning to have my doubts about it. I climb out of the hatch and get another pump and a long hose and electrical wire and proceed to pump out the water. This takes a while and it does not get any warmer in the hatch. When the water level goes down I see that the stuffing box is leaking so I tighten it up and all is well for now.

What will happen next? I wonder.

During this fishing trip I have been trying to learn how to cut the heads off the fish. I have always just taken out the gills so I have to remind myself that I have to cut off the heads. I don't seem to be able to do it very well and get a couple done that I think will just be culls. We also have to clean all the blood out and make sure the lice are removed. After that comes the glazing. We put a garbage bucket down the hatch and pump seawater into it and wait until the water cools down to around 30 degrees. Then I climb down into the hatch and dip each fish once and stack them away in the pens. I keep looking at them wondering if I have enough or too much glaze on the fish.

So up in the cabin the water tank springs a leak, which I have to repair. I dig out the Sikaflex and slap some on and then the hydraulics for the gurdies start to leak. By now nothing surprises me. In all the years I have fished I have never seen so many things go wrong.

Finally I get everything working right and we are catching some fish and everyone is happy. The kids work hard and eat everything in sight. Once in a while I like to have a cookie with my tea so I go to dig out a bag of Dad's Cookies and find it is completely empty. The buggers had eaten them all and put the bag back in the cupboard.

Then DFO closes us down so it is time to take the fish in to unload and find out how we did preparing them for the freezer.

"I want to know what I did wrong with these fish," I tell the grader. After he looks over the fish he tells me they are nice and clean, no blood, and the glaze is good and the heads were cut off good.

"You only did one thing wrong," he says, "and that is no big deal. You don't need to cut the throat all the way up." So after all my fretting and worrying we got an excellent grade. What started out to be a trip from hell turned out to be not so bad.

Tuna 1998

I DECIDE I WANT TO TRY FOR TUNA SO I BUY SOME JIGS AND
whatnot and head to the tuna fishing grounds. I have Yvonne's
daughter Theda with me and my grandson Glen. We anchor at
Cox Island off Cape Scott and the next morning head offshore
and run for three hours when we stop and set the gear. I don't
have any idea what I am doing but I am sure I will learn. We troll
along at five or six knots for hours and at last we get a tuna on; I
lose it at the stern of the boat.

Then a big pod of Pacific white-sided dolphins shows up and
plays around the boat for about two hours. The kids are having a
ball up on the bow screaming at them.

Nothing to do and I don't see another boat anywhere so I
decide to run into Sea Otter Cove for the night, but it is 35 miles
away, four hours steady running. We troll for a while and the
next surprise is a big sunfish, just a big, thin, white, round blob.
Just as we are picking up the gear a second big tuna hooks on
so I turn back, but no more. Off to San Jo Bay, anchor and plan
what we will do the next day. We are going to run out the 45
miles to the 1,000-fathom edge and give it a try. We are up and
running by dawn and I see John Demidoff on *Solemar* on his
way, too. I give him a call and he tells me he still has 50 miles to
go. *Gawd*, I think to myself, *do I really have to go that far?* So I
tailgate John all the way out.

After six hours of running we put the gear out and troll for five
hours and at last we get a tuna. We end up with four for the day
and I think, *what a way to make a dollar.* Come dark, we pick up
the gear and... drift. It's a real nice night with no wind and we
are 72 miles from shore.

Up at first light and jigs in the water but no fish, so I phone John and he tells me I should travel at six knots, not three as I had been, and also how to set my lines. I had the gear dragging too deep in the water and it should have been shallower. It takes a while but we change everything around to his way and we start to catch a few fish. I remembered someone had told me that you had to pick up the stabilizers because they scare the tuna. So we pick up the stabilizers and right away we get seven tuna on the gear. We sure are rolling in the swell though and the kids don't like it much, so I put the stabilizers back over again. We are not rolling now but not catching fish either. I would rather be rolling and catching fish than just sitting here.

We go along for a time with me bitching about no fish and Theda looks at me and says, "We will catch some soon."

Lo and behold we get ten real fast. So I go to put them down the hatch and I see water down there. I turn on the bilge pump and no water comes out, the hose is frozen again. Plan B for the frozen hose is grab the spare pump, a long wire and a long hose and go down the hatch with the pump and put it in the bilge. This one's not pumping either, but then it starts up with a rush and the long wire is ripped out of my hand and gets hooked around the shaft. The pump hooks the bonding wire (a three-eighths-inch copper wire that unites all the stray electricity in the boat) so the bonding wire and the pump wire and the switch all get wrapped around the turning shaft. In no time all the wire is wrapped around the shaft and is hitting the nuts on the stuffing box, where the shaft goes through the hull to the propeller outside the boat. All in all it is one hell of a mess. I have to turn the motor off and we drift a while and I cut all the wire off the shaft. I am a raving maniac by the time I finish this and burst out of the hatch in search of the third pump. This pump stops after I get it going, then Glen drops the hose on my head, which was full of water from the pumping. I am not a happy guy as I come out of the hatch for the tenth time.

For now, I have the bilge pumped out but with the nuts of the stuffing box loosened from being whapped by the wrapped wire, there is a steady leak so I will have to pump every four hours, day and night.

About this time the compressor that keeps the freezer cold starts acting up and making strange noises. So I dive down into the engine room to see if I can calm it down but it's no good. I shut it off and curse the whole outfit, wishing I had never put in a freezer.

Between trying to keep the boat afloat 100 miles offshore, and keep the compressor happy, and learn how to catch tuna, I was a madman.

John calls me up on the radio. "Bill," he says, "if the dolphins follow you, you won't catch any tuna, they get scared away."

I look out the back door and as far as my eye can see, there are dolphins, hundreds of them. They come right alongside the boat and I see they are northern right whale dolphins. Of all the boats in the area, why did they have to choose mine to come and play around? But play they did, for over an hour. Nothing to do but look at them closely; they are about five feet long and have no dorsal fin, like little black sausages. I figure there must be over a thousand of them. The kids get a kick out of watching them and they sure put on a good show. Then the west wind picks up and along with it the swell so we pick up the gear and drift while I go look for a nut to replace a cracked one in the stuffing box.

While I am down in the bow looking for a nut, Theda sticks her head down and says, "Billy, you gotta come look." So I climb up the ladder and there are five sperm whales right by the boat. They lie there like big logs so I watch them for a bit then go back to looking for a nut.

I have lots of nuts on board, but no five-eighths-inch nuts so I go look to see if I can rob one from somewhere. I find one on the bolt that holds the trolling pole. I take it off, and it is a long nut. I have to hacksaw it in half so I will have one for the pole and one for the stuffing box.

Everyone should try holding a nut securely, in a rolling boat, and cutting it in half, square and straight, with a hacksaw. Fun. But by God I did it. Now I have two nuts, one for the pole and one for the stuffing box. At least the pole won't fall down and the stuffing box won't leak… I hope.

After this long, eventful, stressful day, we climb into the bunks. Theda asks me what I think about the wind.

"It will be fine," I tell her. And it was. A good night out here makes one feel free as the wind.

I am up at daylight and put the gear out and get two tuna right away. The kids get up and we see the same five sperm whales and get a good close look at them. They sure are big.

"I want to see a sea turtle," says Theda. By God, an hour later a big sea turtle appears off the bow. This turtle was seven feet long, huge, and likely weighed about 600 pounds. The kids spend most of the day hanging over the bow, where they also see one big shark, some small blue sharks and three sunfish.

So we decide to head for shore and on the way, three Dall's porpoises follow for a long time. I run close by Beresford Island to show the kids the sea lions and set the anchor at Lanz Island. We row in for a shore break and the kids run around looking for glass balls or any other interesting thing but we don't find anything.

On the way to Port McNeill the next day we see several grey whales by Cache Creek and a huge pod of orcas in Goletas Channel. There are over a hundred so I am pretty sure it is the group called the "offshore orcas."

"No one will believe we saw so many things," Glen says. I will say the kids are both good sailors and good deckhands. Anyone who has never been out of sight of land, drifting under a starry sky, has missed a very beautiful experience, although I admit I like to see another mast light on the horizon.

I saw there is a lot more comradeship among the tuna fishers than among salmon fishermen. Everyone is out to help and tells how many fish he has and where he got them. But it works both ways; it's too big an ocean to try to find the tuna by yourself.

Tuna 1999

AUGUST 27, 1999, WE ARE HEADING UP GOLETAS CHANNEL, PROB-ably for the last time, going to try and catch some tuna. Theda's mom, Yvonne, is my deckhand on this trip. As I sit and watch the shoreline pass I can't help but think of the years gone by when me and my deckhand would be heading down the channel, along with all the other fishing boats, with a full load of sockeye, or coho or springs, everyone happy and talking on the phone.

Those were happy times, with everyone making money and eager to get back out for another load—which may be part of the reason why we are where we are today. Life can take some funny turns. We go along thinking what we are doing is alright, when all of a sudden we realize we are part of the problem.

It's more than sixty years since I pulled my first big spring over the side of my boat, and a lot of water has gone under my keel since that day. I have seen a lot of fishermen come and go in that time. Some made good and some went broke. I was one of the lucky ones. At one time I was a so-called highliner, and I was told many times I could "catch fish in a bathtub."

Now, for many of the fishermen who started when I did, those days are gone.

Going by Bull Harbour, I think of the time when there were three troll camps and over 200 trollers, mostly small day trollers who sold their catch each night. The owners of these trollers were a bunch of rugged individuals who fished alone and never took a deckhand. The reason for this was the price they got for their catch: it was so low that there was no money to pay a deckhand. Generally the boats were too small for two people anyway.

Back in the '40s, if you made $1,000 for the season you had done well. In 1982, I quit and went home on August 13 with $72,000. Now we never get enough fishing days to make it pay.

Going over Nahwitti Bar on our way to Sea Otter Cove the sea is calm, just a low roll, and no wind. It seems so strange not to see another boat. When we get to Sea Otter I can't believe how much kelp there is; it's solid all across the entrance. My guess is that boats going in and out of the cove used to keep the kelp down.

Yvonne and I spend two days trying to find some "tuna water" but no luck. Three days and we never see another boat, nor sperm whales, sea turtles or sunfish. It's a big ocean to find yourself all alone in, and hear no one on the radio. I tell Yvonne all about everything we saw and everything that went wrong on the last trip with Theda and Glen.

We shut down to drift the night about 50 miles offshore. Coast Guard comes on with a gale warning so we decide to run partway in. About two in the morning the wind begins to howl in the rigging so we head for Cape Cook. We make Cape Cook at daylight and plan to anchor there, but Coast Guard comes on again with a southwest gale warning. We keep on running, headed for the safe anchorage of Sea Otter Cove; five more hours of a very rolly ride.

We spend the day exploring and hiking out to Lowrie Bay and finally the wind goes down, but there is still a big swell running. We leave Sea Otter Cove but it is still too rough to go offshore and the forecast doesn't sound that good, plus there are no other boats around. We decide to head for home. On the way to Cape Scott a stabilizer line breaks so I anchor again and have to climb the mast to tie on a new one. With the boat rolling heavily like hell, it's not a fun job, but it is all part of the game.

We caught only four tuna, but we made it home safe and sound. I gave Yvonne three and one to my daughter Patty.

That was my last trip out to the west coast of Vancouver Island, and Yvonne's last fishing trip with me.

Sockeye 2000

WELL, I DID NOT EXPECT ANY FISHING TIME IN THIS YEAR BUT all of a sudden DFO gives us an opening so I round up the deck-hands, my other grandson, Derek, and Theda, and away we go.

Theda Miller holds a big sockeye. PHOTO BY DEREK HODDINOTT

We leave home bright and early and get the gear out about 9 a.m. off Port Hardy Airport and troll west.

Anyone who has fished for sockeye knows the fish bite best trolling west and it is not long before we catch a few. It is just enough to get us excited but then we go for hours without a bite. We try fishing deeper but then we catch them on the top lure. We try fast, we try slow, but no bite. The deckhands are eager to pull some fish but the hooks all come up empty. They look at me and say, "Where are the fish?"

I say, "If I knew I would be there."

We troll west all day because we never get anything to turn back on and finally it is time to pick up and go anchor at the end of a very poor day.

I spend most of the next day in the wheelhouse tying gear and watching the radar because it is foggy. About ten times that day I am called outside to look at a fish or solve some problem like a snap through a block that got there all on its own, and when I ask how did that get there the reply is always the same, "I don't know."

Day two Derek cuts his finger and he is leaking blood all over. Little Doctor Theda wants to put a Band-Aid on it but Derek wants nothing to do with a Band-Aid so we have blood all over. Day four, Derek gets constipated and spends most of the day in the head and the rest of the day farting and belching. In fact they both do a lot of belching. Derek is very competitive and tries to get his side of the gear out before Theda but most times she beats him.

We go down to Blackfish Sound to try our luck but all there is are pinks so back to Scarlett Point we go. Turns out it had been a good day at Scarlett Point for the other boats so we missed the best day. But that's fishing. We stay at Scarlett Point for a few days then we hear that the price of pinks has gone up to thirty cents a pound, so we go back to Blackfish Sound to get a load, but when we get there, guess what? No pinks.

All in all we had a lot of fun and made a few bucks and had no major problems, so I call that a good trip.

Sockeye 2010

IN FEBRUARY OF 2010 I WAS IN PORT MCNEILL ONE DAY AND I met a friend from Sointula. We got to talking about the sockeye and he wanted to know what I thought the run would be.

"You better get a good net because there is going to be a big run," I said. "I think there will be over twenty-five million fish."

He just laughed but said, "You have made my day."

I ran into another man who was going to sell his licence because he didn't think there would be any sockeye to catch. The main reason for this way of thinking was because in 2009 DFO (now called Fisheries and Oceans Canada) forecast nine million sockeye but just a little over a million returned. Anyway I talked him into keeping his licence for one more year.

So it came August 1 and the sockeye started to show in good numbers and I had my boat all ready to go. DFO announced it was going to open for trolling and we would be allowed to catch 1,300 each so we went and caught our 1,300 and came home.

Three days later DFO announced we could catch another 1,200 so we went and caught them and then DFO announced we could just keep fishing until we caught 5,500, but we quit when we had 3,800.

It turned out it was by far the largest run in recorded history. The DFO test boat had 96,000 fish on its best day. Catches of that size were unheard of before this run. I know I had never seen that many sockeye in my lifetime.

Word spread that I had predicted a big run of sockeye for 2010. First CBC Radio called and wanted to interview me about the salmon run, so I told why I had predicted that big run. Then the BC Salmon Commission called and wanted to know why I had predicted that big run.

I have kept my own logbooks since 1958 and I know how many fish I have caught every year. In light of the fact that sockeye spawn at three, four or five years old, some years there are three- and four-year-old salmon returning and some years four- and five-year-olds.

Only once in every sixty years do all three ages return in the same year. It looked to me like 2010 was that year.

Observations on the Department of Fisheries and Oceans

THIS IS ABOUT WHAT VARIOUS DFO RULINGS OVER THE YEARS have done to manage the salmon stocks on the BC coast and the impact they've had on the salmon and on the small commercial fishers. I began commercial trolling in 1942 with a rowboat, and through the years worked my way up to bigger and better boats. When I started, a licence cost one dollar and allowed you to keep any species of fish you caught. In 1951 I got my first powered boat and at that time the commercial season opened on February 1 and closed December 1. I never fished in the winter but would begin June 15 to fish for chinook salmon in Blackfish Sound. It is in Fisheries Management Area 12, which covers all the area between just north of Kelsey Bay and as far northwest as Seymour Inlet.

As noted earlier, Area 12 at one time was the most productive area on the BC coast. It includes Knight Inlet, Kingcome Inlet and Wakeman, Bond and Thompson Sounds, and hundreds of thousands of fish pass through on their way down Johnstone Strait to the Fraser River as well.

I lived in Blackfish Sound so, like many of the trollers who lived all along the coast, I fished close to where I lived. In the early part of the season I fished only chinook (or spring) salmon, catching anywhere from ten to twenty a day, with twenty being a real good day's catch.

Blackfish Sound was always noted as a prime chinook fishing area but in the early years there were no camps open to sell your catch to until July 1, so no one fished the early runs of chinook. There was a gillnet camp in Alert Bay run by BC Packers and they would buy troll-caught fish but did not make a habit of it, and it was only open four days a week like the gillnet fishery.

I would fish for one day and the next morning and then I would run to Alert Bay to sell my catch. The gillnet camp had no ice and my boat was too small to pack ice anyway. In 1963 Dan Sutherland's camp at Simoom Sound opened on April 15. By then I had a bigger boat (33-foot *Dynamite II*) and I could pack ice, which I got from old seine boats such as *London III* and *White Wave*. They would bring the ice up from Vancouver on their way to Alert Bay to prepare the boat for seine fishing. So I began to fish from April 15, and I also began to fish up the inlets instead of just in Blackfish Sound.

In the '50s and '60s there was one Fisheries officer stationed in Alert Bay and he had one assistant. There were also ten patrolmen in the area. The patrolman's job started June 15 and went until November 15. His job was to walk the streams and rivers, cut trails, count fish and watch for poachers. The Fisheries officer was out on the fishing grounds a lot in those days. His job was to check on the patrolmen, get their reports and find out how all the runs were showing. While he was making his rounds he would check in with any fishermen in the area and ask how we were doing. He always asked what our thoughts were on how the runs were showing up.

This was a real good system because we were on the grounds every day and had a good idea of how many fish were coming through. There were many guys like me who had fished their home areas for years all along the coast, and we got to know when the runs were due to come in. We could tell by our catches if it was going to be a big run or not.

This system was very beneficial to the management of the fishery and the information was freely shared and the fishermen had a good relationship with the Fisheries officers. We trusted each other and they were open to our suggestions. No one knows better how the runs are looking than the fisherman who is on the grounds every day; it is in his best interest to know this because it is his livelihood.

In the 1960s, DFO hired a lot of men to try to cure the ills of the fishing industry—mainly too many boats chasing too few fish. First Jack Davis took over, and his plan was no boat would be licensed for salmon in 1969 unless it had fished for salmon in 1967 or by September 6, 1968. (A new fisherman could buy out another fisher so that the total number did not increase.) Then came Peter Pearse's report, where he listed all the things that were wrong. Boats were now to be divided into two categories, A and B.

Category A boats were those that had landings in excess of 10,000 pounds, in terms of pink and chum units. At the time much of our poundage was made up of coho, sockeye and chinook so the ruling did not make much sense to me, but that was the new rule.

Category B boats were those that had less than 10,000 pounds in landings of pink and chum.

Only A boats could be retired and replaced by a new boat. B boats could fish but could not be replaced; they could only fish for ten more years and then had to be retired.

Fishing licence fees were to increase to a hundred dollars a year. The money from the increased licence fees would be used to buy back Category A salmon boats out of the industry. In my opinion this was a gross waste of taxpayers' money. Instead, the money should have been used for salmon enhancement to increase the salmon stocks.

That was the beginning of the buyback plan—which, to my mind, was a total farce. By 1972 DFO had bought back 1,000 boats. The plan aimed to reduce the catching power of the fleet and leave more fish for the remaining fishermen. As it turned out, DFO cut the fleet by a quarter but over half the boats that were bought back were low producers.

It has always been known in the fleet that 20 percent of the boats catch 80 percent of the fish. A buyback does not make sense to me because in any other industry or business, if you can't make a go of it and you go broke, the government doesn't come and buy you out. Why do so for the fisherman?

Around this time, many fishermen overspent on and invested in bigger boats, so with bigger boats and a big debt, they had to catch more fish to pay for it. What this boils down to is an over-capitalized fleet.

In 1969 Jack Davis said, "Take your cut now and you will reap the harvest after." In 2009 I was still waiting. However, it could be that the runs of 2010 and 2014 might be considered the harvest reaped from those measures.

After the Davis Plan, DFO hired a man named Wayne Shinners to do a study of the coast. He divided all the areas of the coast into many smaller sub-areas. Area 12 was divided into thirty-six sub-areas. The idea was DFO could open a small sub-area for fishing, which would protect the salmon in other areas. The sub-areas became known as "Shinners cubes." I thought that was a pretty good idea.

Right around this time DFO began to lay off patrolmen and gave the ones left on the job larger areas to look after. They had the patrolmen (and women) working in areas where fishing was in progress, to collect catch figures. They seemed to think that was more important than patrolling the streams, so there was some poaching that went on in the inlets while the patrolmen were busy with the fleet.

The last plan to come along was the Pacific Salmon Revitalization Strategy, or Mifflin Plan. For fishermen, this was the last straw. Mifflin called for more buybacks and area licencing. The fishers had to pick an area and that was where you stayed for the whole season. So there was no more following the salmon as they migrated down the coast. Sometimes when a new plan is put into effect it is kind of hard to swallow, but as time goes by you learn to accept it, and after many years of observation, you may decide it was not such a bad idea.

When licence limitations came along, from the fisherman's point of view things got worse. What this meant was if a fisherman wanted to have a new boat built, it had to be the same tonnage as the one being replaced. Unfortunately this turned out to be a big joke. There were seine boats built from 38-foot gillnetters, for example. There were just so many creative ways a fisherman could get around this ruling, and they did. Some fishermen put in false bulkheads or false floors and then removed them after the measurement had been done.

Next DFO came out with a rule that stated if you were going to build a new boat it had to be the same length as the one you were replacing. This was a farce too, because fishermen then had boats built with a false bow. For instance a guy might get a licence off a

42-foot boat, and then build a boat with a false, or detachable, bow. You take the bow off for measuring, and bolt it back on afterwards. Presto you have a 50-foot boat, which meant you could make a seine boat out of a troller or gillnetter.

With the Mifflin Plan came selective fishing, which meant we had to release non-targeted species, like coho and chinook. This just seemed so odd. After years of fishing chinook and coho it just did not seem right to me to shake them off. At first it was coho because the coho stocks were crashing coastwide. By the mid-'70s the trollers took 44 percent of the salmon catch, and the fleet had gotten so efficient that something really needed to be done.

In the 1980s DFO set a quota for coho on the west coast of Vancouver Island. They set the quota on the previous year's catch though, which happened to be 1.1 million, the largest catch ever up to that point. So for a few years trollers were still fishing in October trying to fill the allowed quota; which is when Minister David Anderson put a moratorium on coho coastwide.

For me, one of the changes I disliked the most was the relationship between Fisheries officers and fishermen. In the old days we used to like to see the DFO officer come aboard, but now they have guns on their hips and they do not take your word—mainly, I guess, because they do not know each fisherman, nor his reputation. One officer we nicknamed "Sockeye Sue" went down the hatch and dug all my big chinooks out of the ice looking for sockeye, because sockeye were closed on this occasion. I asked her if she was going to re-ice the fish and she said no. That was not her job. I ended up having to go deliver early because after she was through I didn't have enough ice to re-ice those fish. This kind of treatment caused us to feel a big loss of respect for DFO officers. Instead of being innocent until proven guilty we were considered guilty until proven innocent.

In 1979 there were only five trollers fishing for chinook in Area 12. I was in Blackfish Sound with one other troller, averaging ten chinook per day. DFO closed all of Area 12 for commercial trolling for the conservation of chinook and Area 12 has never been re-opened for commercial trolling, gillnetting or seining of chinook.

Currently, the coast is divided into three fishing areas. North of Cape Caution has been designated Area F, the west coast of Vancouver Island is Area G and the waters east of Vancouver Island are Area H. This area begins at Pine Island and goes down to the Fraser River. The licence cost jumped to $710, plus $60 for a personal commercial licence and $300.75 for a logbook to record your catch.

I first opted for an Area G licence but changed to an Area H licence later because I had put in my time fishing offshore Vancouver Island and up in the Queen Charlotte Islands, now called Haida Gwaii. Every year I must buy a licence and a logbook and a lot of years we don't get a chance to fish or, if we can, it is only for sockeye, pink and chum. Even if we don't use the logbook we have to send it back before the end of the year. When we do get a chance to fish we have to record all our activities in the logbook, such as what sub-area we are fishing in and how many hours we fished, what time we began and when we quit, how many fish we kept and how many we released and what species. At the end of the day we have to phone in and report what we wrote in the logbook, and we must be certain that both reports are exactly the same. I guess this is doing some good for the salmon. But it sure is hard on us fishermen.

We also have to phone in ahead of time and tell Archipelago Marine what sub-area we are *going* to be fishing in. For example, if we are in sub-area 12-32 and we want to go fish in sub-area 12-34 we have to phone in. Sometimes we have to phone in three or four times a day, but from this, DFO does know in what areas the fish are being caught, and how many.

We are only allowed to keep sockeye, pinks and chum, and have to release coho and chinook. With the Mifflin Plan and selective fishing we also have to have a "revival box." The boxes cost seven hundred dollars and we also have to have a pump to maintain a good constant flow of water at all times. If we get a coho or chinook that is near dead, we put it in the box to help revive it. These boxes work to some degree; I think about 20 percent survive.

Most trollers work the gear quickly; we don't play our fish the way the sport fisherman does. We get them to the boat as fast as possible so most fish are very much alive. If they are hooked through the top of the head or through the eye or the gills they are going to die because they are bleeding. We always try to stay away from where we know there is a non-targeted species.

When Blackfish Sound was closed to commercial trolling in 1979 there were very few sport fishers. We would see a few on the weekend, but now there are many sport fishers there every day. Many of these boats are from fishing lodges. They fish all day from first light to last and they are experts at catching salmon. The point I want to make clear is that when we were commercial fishing chinook salmon, we were only taking ten to twenty a day at the most and we were being checked by DFO on the grounds, and also through our sales slips, and later with hail-ins and logbooks. DFO knew exactly how many fish were being caught. The sport fleet is catching way

This is a pretty big Chinook salmon. PHOTO BY YVONNE MAXIMCHUK

more fish than we ever did and there is no system in place to keep track of the numbers. Sport fishing licences are never tabulated, no Fisheries officers are stopping the sport fishing boats and checking on the catch in the boats, and there are no logbooks to turn in or sales slips or tallies gathered anywhere.

Sport fishing rules state one wild coho per day per fisher, and one hatchery coho with a clipped fin. I have seen many sport fishers catch the one wild one, and then fish all day seeking to catch a hatchery fish. They catch and release a number of wild ones and the released fish have often been worn out while the fisherman played it up to the boat. Somehow they expect the fish will survive and some do, but many die or get eaten by a seal or sea lion after they are released. And many are just considered fair game and taken anyway, because who is watching?

Why don't sport fishers have to have a revival box just like the commercial fisher? That would be fair. And if it is of real value in reviving a tired-out salmon, that would be fair to the fish, too.

I believe the use of natural bait like herring and anchovies should be outlawed for the sport fisher. The use of herring by commercial trollers was outlawed in Blackfish Sound over seventy years ago. Even when I was a boy, if a troller was found to be using herring, the other trollers would run him off the grounds. It looks to me like that might be an effective method for conservation of salmon stocks.

In 1996, the Pacific Policy Roundtable was formed to address conservation and allocation issues amongst all the commercial gear types, plus Aboriginal and sport fishing. Members representing the troll fleet recommended implementing a quota system on a trial basis. When this system was first brought in, under the Mifflin Plan, I did not know what to think, but now I do believe the quota system is helping and will continue to help build up the runs in the years to come. It has also done away with the competition to be a highliner—everyone is equal. There is one thing wrong with it, though. I think if you have a quota, you should be the one to fish it and not be allowed to lease it. Being allowed to lease a quota has made for a lot of armchair fishermen.

Just for example, say a man has a halibut quota of 4,000 pounds and he leases it for three dollars per pound and the man who is fishing it gets four-fifty a pound; the man who is sitting at home is making the money while the fisherman and his crew are making very little. This does not seem fair to me when it is the fishing crew who are out doing the work in all kinds of weather.

The buyback plan, which we hated at first, has done some good because for many years, as Pearse noted, there were too many boats chasing too few fish. I guess a lot of these fishermen would have just gone broke without the buyback. There were over 6,000 fishing boats when the buyback plans were first introduced. Now there are around 2,200. Troller numbers have been reduced from 1,900 to around 500 these days.

DFO, or Fisheries and Oceans Canada, as it is now known, should hire more patrol officers and put them back to work up all the inlets and salmon-bearing streams. The other very important change is that FOC should take a far stronger stand against damage to salmon-bearing streams through logging practices.

And finally, I believe that although Port McNeill is largely considered a logging community, fishers also spend a lot of money in the town. It would be good for the economy for the town and area to diversify and invest in good facilities to support fishing activity. As it is now, prawns, crab, cod, salmon, clams, sea urchins and sea cucumbers are all unloaded there and the unloading facilities are quite poor. Port McNeill would benefit from a good fish unloading dock, net rack float and a small ice plant.

These are just my thoughts, after seventy years as a salmon fisherman.

CHAPTER TWO

OLD-TIME FISHERMEN I HAVE KNOWN

HERE ARE SOME OF THE MEN I GOT TO KNOW AT OUR CAMP IN Freshwater Bay every year. They would show up around the first of July, after they had fished for bluebacks in "the gulf," which is what they called the Gulf of Georgia.

ONE OF THE FIRST TO SHOW UP WAS **BEN BACHUS** ON HIS boat *Quinty*. Ben was a nice fellow but a real loner. Some of the other fishermen called him "Backhouse Benny" or "Old KaPuff and a Half." He always wore a visor hat with no top, just the visor, to protect his eyes from the sun. His boat was always clean and tidy. He first came to Blackfish in 1919 but I didn't get to know him until 1943. Ben's boat was powered with a 7 hp Britt gas engine. One day while working on his engine he showed me the spark plug he was cleaning and told me it was eighteen years old. I've seen a lot of spark plugs since then but never one like that.

Ben was a bit deaf and used a hearing aid. It was the first hearing aid I had ever seen. It had a big plug that went in the ear and a wire that ran to a small box in his shirt pocket. The box had dials on it to turn it up or down or shut it off. When I would stop to talk to Ben he would first talk real loud, then he would turn on the hearing aid and talk real low.

When Ben came in with his catch we could always tell where he had been fishing. If he had big springs we knew he had been fishing Flower Island and if he had big coho, it had to have been at the Merry-Go-Round.

Unlike most fishermen, Ben lived year-round on his boat. He tied up at Benson Shipyard in Vancouver. The last year Ben fished was 1960, when he was eighty years old.

ART FLUGHAM WAS A TALL MAN AND RAIL-THIN. HE HAD BLACK hair and everyone called him "Tall Dark." Art travelled in his boat *Artful* with two other boats, and we called them the Three Musketeers.

The second Musketeer was **Jake Damer** on *Jakes Tub* and the third was **Gordon Beurkholts** on the *Nah Hoh Ta*. All their boats were small and haywire and Art and Jake never caught any fish, although Gordon was a good fisherman and caught lots of coho. They used to go and fish at Jeannette Islands in July and August and then come to Blackfish Sound for September. Art called them Starvation Islands. I don't know why they stayed at the Jeannettes when there were no fish.

But that was the way it was with lots of fishermen. They would like a place that was close to a good anchorage and that they got to know real well. Most years it paid off but some years the fish did not show.

One year Art came to Blackfish Sound at the end of August. He told me he had only five dollars left in his pocket after two months of fishing. He didn't know if he should buy some gas and go home, or get some tobacco and stay fishing for a while. There was a big run of coho and everyone was doing well so Art stayed and his first day fishing he had fifty coho. He was one happy guy that night—he made more money in one day than he made in two weeks at Jeannette Islands.

One day there was a gale of west wind blowing and no boats went out. Over forty boats were tied to our dock, tied six deep, and Art was third boat out from the dock. As the story goes, Art woke up and heard the wind and he turned up his haywire old oil stove, put the coffee pot on and fell asleep again. When he woke up the stove was glowing red hot and in a panic he took his pillow and threw it on the stove.

Pretty quick there was smoke curling out around the door and windows. Ken Slater was the first to see smoke and came out of his boat, *Wahkana Bay*, with a foam- blowing fire extinguisher. He was pulling on his pants as he bolted out of his boat and while he was climbing up on the boat next to the dock, his pants fell off. Ken made it to Art's boat, opened the door and let fly with the foam, just at the same moment Art was reaching to open his door from the inside. He got the foam right in the face so he backed up quick and made for the hatch in the cabin roof.

Old **Wes Summers** on the *Standby* was tied alongside and he yanked open the hatch and dumped a tub of water down it just as Art was reaching up. Poor old Art came crawling out of his cabin door on his hands and knees soaking wet and covered in foam and feathers. He sure was a sorry sight in his dirty old long johns, but at least neither his boat nor any other got burned up that day.

JOE MACWHINNIE WAS A VERY BIG IRISHMAN BUT HIS BOAT, named *She*, was real small, only 26 feet long, powered with a 4 hp Easthope gas engine. Joe only trolled in Parson Bay and only fished for coho. When he came in to sell his catch, Joe went and

Joe MacWhinnie sent this photo to my mom in July 1944. He is on the left. He always called me the beast or brute and I can't blame him. I must have made his life miserable. PHOTO COURTESY OF JAE PROCTOR

tied up and never came out of his boat unless he needed something from the store. The rest of the time we never saw him on the dock. Joe hated kids. He always called me "the beast" or "brute," so naturally this called for some action on my part. When he was sleeping I would tie many knots in his lines or I would run past his boat making lots of noise, but Mom gave me heck so I had to stop.

JIMMY DENNIS ON *BLUEBELL* WAS A REAL NICE MAN BUT VERY dirty—his boat was one of the dirtiest of the fleet. When I was a

Jimmy Dennis washing his blue jeans, with a little help from me and my old dog Mickey in 1942. PHOTO BY JAE PROCTOR

small boy Jimmy would put his boat on the beach by our house and live in it all winter. He did that for a few winters until he moved into one of the cabins. One winter Joe MacWhinnie moved in with him. They had been friends for years but when they lived in the cabin they got into a big fight because Joe was real clean and Jimmy was so dirty. After the fight they both took off for Vancouver.

The next year when Jimmy came up he had a new boat called *Zev*. He'd go and gillnet for sockeye in Rivers Inlet and at the end of July he would return to Blackfish Sound and troll until October. Jimmy would leave all his gillnet gear in our basement; net guard and stern roller and the thing he used for pulling his nets before gillnet drums were invented. I have never seen another of these. It was a kind of homemade capstan winch and was mounted on the rear end out of a car and it sat upright. It was about a foot deep and two feet across and looked like two basins bolted together, bottom to bottom. This was powered with shafts and belts from the main engine. He'd put the end of the net in it and, as it turned, pull the net in hand over hand. And sadly, he and Joe never did get to be friends again.

ANOTHER FISHERMAN, **HUGH MCHARDY,** HAD A BOAT NAMED *N.M.S.* and everyone called him "No More Salmon." My mom called him "Fuzzy Bunny" because he had long hair growing out of his ears and nose. Hugh went barefoot all the time and always wore a long black woollen coat, which looked real odd with his bare feet poking out. Hugh's boat was always really messy with junk all over the deck and it smelled bad. When there were a lot of boats tied up at our camp and they had to raft together no one would tie up to Hugh's boat because it was too hard to get across to the dock. Hugh never caught many fish because his gear was real haywire and he just kind of stooged around out offshore. He never fished among the other boats. I don't think he could see very well as he wore real thick glasses and he always had trouble making a landing.

I MET A BIG MAN CALLED **GEORGE SWEET** IN 1948. HE WAS seventy years old and I was fourteen. His boat, named *Bridgewater*, was a big boat for that era; a real heavy boat 38 feet long powered with a two-cylinder Vivian gas engine. George kept his boat nice and clean and took very good care of it. He never caught many fish because he never fished long hours; he would go out real early but most days he would be in by noon.

One of the odd things about George was he did all his cooking out on deck on a two-burner Coleman gas stove. I used to sit and talk to George and watch him cook his supper. Everything was cooked in a frying pan. His stove was old and did not burn too well so George would stand there with a squirt can full of gas. Just as the stove was about to go out George would give it a squirt from the can. When he would squirt the stove, the gas at the end of the squirt can would catch on fire and he would pinch the flame out with his fingers. I think he did his cooking on deck so he could throw the stove overboard if it caught on fire.

George fished Blackfish Sound until he was eighty years old and he never had a fire while I knew him, and he never seemed to hurt his fingers pinching out the flame. George used to eat a lot of onions and one thing I remember he told me was when you peel an onion, always take the first layer off. I still do this today.

I FIRST MET **ALLEN SOUCH SR.** IN 1966 WHEN I WAS FISHING in Kingcome Inlet. His boat was called *Northern Sea*. We talked on the phone (the VHF radio) every day so I got to know him real well. We would anchor together at night if we were in the same area. Allen liked to fish in Kwatsi Bay in Tribune Channel. Kwatsi means "piss pot" in the local Native language, so when I would phone him he would say, "I am down in the pot." Back in the 1960s Kwatsi Bay was a good place to fish big springs as they would stop there to feed and rest on their way up to Knight Inlet to spawn.

Every year on the twentieth of June we would go to fish Blackfish Sound. We'd fish along the shores of Swanson Island and Flower Island and anchor in Freshwater Bay at night. We fished together from 1966 until 1979, when DFO closed Blackfish Sound for commercial trolling. We only fished the flood and together we'd anchor in Breakfast Bay when the tide was not right for fishing.

Once we got the anchor down and tied our boats together we would have breakfast, which was usually bacon and eggs or hot cakes. Allen loved red kidney beans fried in bacon fat. We liked to sit there and wait for the tide to slack off and watch for the back eddy to form. Then we'd go back out and fish the low-water slack, follow the flood down to Flower Island and then fish there. If the tide was right we'd anchor in Freshwater Bay waiting for the evening bite.

There are three days in every ten days when the tide is right at first light. The first one up the shore of Swanson Island on those mornings gets the best catch. So when the tide was right Allen and I would take turns. Allen would go one morning and I would go the next. On days when the fishing was poor Allen would phone me and say, "I think it's time to go and have a cup of coffee and a cupcake." There was nothing Allen liked better on those days than sitting on the hatch of my boat, *Twilight Rock*, drinking coffee and telling stories. This was a great way of life—the fishing was good and Allen was a great guy and a good fishing buddy.

VIC COBBLER WAS A TROLLER AND LINGCOD FISHERMAN. VIC was like a lot of the trollers of that era: they never caught many fish because their boats and gear were really haywire. They also pulled their lines by hand. His boat was named *Maxine* and it was powered with a one-cylinder Atlas Imperial gas engine. The *Maxine* was like a lot of boats in the 1930s and '40s: it had no wheelhouse, just a low trunk cabin with a sliding hatch and a low door leading to steps to get into the cabin. This meant you had to stand outside to steer, or lean on the hatch. The steering wheel was on the back of the cabin and there was a pole to shift gears and a string or wire to speed up or slow down the engine.

Most of the old one-cylinder engines had a poor reverse. So when old Vic came into our dock he would put the engine in reverse over 100 feet from the dock, but the boat never slowed down. Old Vic would be leaning on the hatch with his pipe in his mouth trying to speed the engine up, but most times nothing happened. All of a sudden he would spring to life and toss me a line so I could wrap it around a post on the float and stop the boat. We had the post put in just for this purpose as a lot of the boats were like Vic's.

Vic was a real loner but he sure liked to talk. He always talked with his pipe in his mouth and he had a really high-pitched voice. He always started with, "Well now, I was a figuring…" He would say, "Well now, I was a figuring the coho will show on the full moon tides." And most times he was right.

Or, if he was cod fishing he would say, "Well now, I was a figuring the cod are gone where all good cod go—east of the Rockies."

Vic spent the winters in Alert Bay. One winter he took to log salvaging and sold his logs to the local mill. One day he got the tow line caught in the propeller. The wind came up and the old *Maxine* went ashore on the point of Alert Bay. Vic managed to get it towed off but it was beyond repair so the folks in the Bay got together and bought him another boat. Vic was a steam engineer by trade, so he got a job running the steam retorts at the cannery in Alert Bay till the cannery closed down. By this time Vic was getting along in years, so he just lived on his boat till he passed away.

HANS ECKHOFF FIRST CAME TO OUR CAMP IN 1945 IN HIS boat *Poseidon*. This was a nice boat and he took good care of it and was a good fisherman. Hans would fish long hours and in all kinds of weather. He was high boat almost every day. He was really competitive and did not like to be beaten. I must say, there are a lot of us like that.

When I started to fish with the *Aye Aye* in 1952, my first big boat, I started to give Hans some competition because I knew the area and the tides so well. Hans and I would pass on the grounds and holler or give a hand up of how the day was going. Mostly we would tell how many big springs we had, but some days we would give our coho numbers.

I remember one day in mid-August, Hans passed me by and showed me five fingers meaning he had five big springs. I only had two, so this called for some action. Usually by mid-August I had taken most of my spring spoons off and had put coho spoons on. So off come the coho spoons and on go my shiny spring spoons, hanging perfectly, just for this occasion. I just could not let Hans beat me in my own backyard. Besides, big springs were my speciality.

There are two times on the tide when the big springs bite: halfway through the flood tide and then just as the tide starts to ebb out of Knight Inlet. So I get my gear all set and head straight to Spring Salmon Bay just when the tide is starting to flood. I trolled along the big kelp patch and in about an hour got one big spring.

Well, I just kept circling around the bay and when the tide was just right, I got three more really big ones. Then I had to wait for the ebb out of Knight Inlet and as soon as the kelp came up, I was right there and I got four more big springs.

Now I had ten big smileys on board and I went out of my way to pass Hans and see how many he had. He gives me the sign that he had six and I said, "I got ten." He threw up his hands and yelled back, "Yi, yi, yi," and went back into his cabin. Most times Hans was hard to beat. I know I had to work harder to beat him, but competition is what makes a good fisherman.

Hans fished Blackfish Sound till 1960 when he sold *Poseidon* and bought the *Essie T*. He went off to fish Bull Harbour and I never saw him after that. Hans most likely never knew it, but he made me a better fisherman because I had to keep my gear in good shape and work longer hours. I learned from Hans that the fisherman who keeps his gear in the water from daylight till dark and keeps the hooks clean and sharp will end up being top boat most days.

IRVING JOHANSON HAD A NICE TROLLER NAMED *VIOLA*; HE came to Blackfish Sound in the mid-1970s, new at the fishing

OLD-TIME FISHERMEN I HAVE KNOWN •

game. He was fishing out of Mitchell Bay and so was I. When we went in to deliver at night Irving would be there on the scow to meet us and he always had a cup of coffee in his hand.

At that time there were a lot of pinks and sockeye around so we would have 500 to 600 on deck every night, and every night Irving would look at them and say, "Got a few today, eh." So after a while I got to know him a bit and asked him how he was doing and he said he was only getting thirty or forty a day so I said, "Can I look at your gear?"

"Sure," he says, so I went over and I could not believe what he was dragging around expecting to catch fish. The next day I quit fishing early so I could work on his gear.

I cut all his gear off of one side and set it up just like mine and I told him to watch where I was fishing. The next night when I went in to deliver there was Irving standing on the scow with his coffee cup in his hand and a grin on his face. I knew he had got some fish. As it turned out he had got over 300 and he was sure one happy guy. He fished Blackfish Sound till it was closed to all fishing so I never saw much of Irving after that.

I FIRST MET **JIMMY KASK** IN 1945; HE HAD A REAL NICE BOAT for that era. It was 36 feet long, named *Mary K*. He had *Mary K* for a few years then he got another one named *Swing*, also a very nice boat. He always went north to fish and he would stop and fish coho in Blackfish Sound in September. Then he got another boat named *Erin* and he started to fish Kingcome Inlet and Knight Inlet. He only had *Erin* for a short time and then got a real big boat named *Regal One*.

Jimmy was kind of a loner and never teamed up with other fishermen much. I never saw him for years until one day I was

Jimmie Kask, skipper of Ann Gale. PHOTO BY SUSAN PEARSON

fishing up Knight Inlet and there he was. I was glad to see him so we anchored together and had a good b.s. about the old days in Blackfish Sound. Jimmy was a good fisherman and took good care of his boats. He loved to fish for spring salmon up in the inlets and for the big coho late in the fall. When DFO closed all the inlets and Blackfish Sound, Jimmy went north again so I didn't see him for several more years until one day I was in Port Hardy and there was Jimmy with a brand new boat named *Ann Gale*. Jimmy was a good shipwright and used to work at Sather Boat Works in the winter and that is where he built the *Ann Gale*. The last time I saw Jimmy he was getting along in years so he would just fish out of Port Hardy and out at the Gordon Group.

CULLY HUNTLEY WAS A TROLLER, TRAPPER AND HAND LOG-
ger. He had a nice little boat named *Tide Rip*. Cully was a big,
powerful man but he had lost his testicles when he was sixteen
years old. He said his gun went off while he was crawling under
a barbwire fence and shot them off.

So because of this he never had to shave and he had real baggy
skin that was almost white. He always wore pants that were too
big for him so a lot of people called him "Old Baggy Ass." Cully
would troll in the summertime, and he only fished for big springs.
He fished most of the time at Card Point. Every other day he
would come to our camp to sell his catch. He always covered the
fish with kelp to keep them cool and damp. When Cully would
come in some of the other fishers would come to watch him unload his catch.

Some would ask him where he got all the big springs and he
would say, "Up in the salal bush," then he would laugh. One day
he came in and there were big wads of moss hanging from the tips
of his trolling poles. Someone asked him how he got the moss
on his poles and he said, "I got too close to the salal bush." Cully
had a real high-pitched voice and a squeaky laugh. He loved to
tell stories and laughed like heck at his own jokes.

Cully had a floathouse and lived part-time in Belleisle Sound.
When he went trapping he would move to Wakeman Sound
where his trapline was. He also hand logged in Wakeman. Cully
was a good hunter—he used to hunt deer up the mountains in
Wakeman. He also liked to hunt ducks and geese and had a trail
on Swanson Island where he would come to hunt. We called it
"Cully's slaughterhouse."

During the war you had to have a permit to buy liquor. Cully
had a dog named Sam so he got a permit for Sam and he would

say proudly, "The only dog on the BC Coast with a liquor permit, Sam Huntley." When trapping was over he would hand log till fishing time and then move his house back into Belleisle for the summer. Cully was the only one I knew who could guddle for trout. He would lie on the bank of a stream with his arm in the water and wait for a trout to swim over and he would grab it by the tail.

As Cully got older he got a bit fat and because he had baggy skin, he would get blisters in the crack of his butt when he went hand logging. This must have hurt like heck, so he made what he called his chafing stick. He had it all curved to fit in his crack and he would tie it in place when he went to work. I saw the stick hanging in his house and asked him what it was, and he told me it was his "chiffing stick"; it was worn real smooth and was stained a bit.

When the *Tide Rip* got old he sold it and bought the *Atom* from John Kàrten. He then took the fish patrol job in Wakeman and Kingcome in the summer and then took camp watch jobs in the wintertime. In 1957 he was watching a camp in Simoom Sound and they found him dead on his boat. He was eighty years old.

A MAN CALLED **GEORGE NELSON** CAME TO BLACKFISH SOUND in 1919 with a rowboat and hand trolled in what he called "the little merry-go-round," along the west shore of Cedar Island. He would fish the flood tide then go sell his catch at Freshwater Bay, then go back to his camp on a little island next to Cedar Island. He also fished Trainer Pass between Crib and Eden Islands, when the tides were right for there. He would sell this catch at Cullen Harbour. I don't know how long he hand trolled but he came to our camp in

On the Echo Bay dock, George Nelson gives another fisherman a haircut alongside his boat Manita. PHOTO COURTESY OF MARLENE MACLAREN

1940 in his 32-foot troller *Manita*, a real nice boat for that era. His wife Lottie was with him and they fished from our camp until 1962 so I got to know them really well.

Some years in August we would get a lot of northwest wind, which could blow for up to five or six days. While it was blowing George would fish in Fife Sound for coho and go into Echo Bay to wait for the wind to die down. George was a good fisherman but he never fished long hours. He'd come in every day around two or three o'clock. He had one spot at the dock that he liked and tied to for years. The reason he liked this spot so much was because he and Lottie ate rockfish every day, so as soon as he was tied up, over went the line, baited with salmon roe. He would catch three copper rockfish and fillet them so there was dinner, every night.

George never talked or mixed with the other fishermen much but Lottie made up for it. She always had her head out the wheelhouse window chatting to anyone who came along. When she came up to our store she always complained about the price of things. My mom would get mad as hell at her, but it went on like that for years.

NORWEGIAN **JOHN WOLFF** WAS A HIGHLINE HALIBUT FISHerman on a boat named *Capella One*, and I used to like to listen to him talking on the old AM phone. His conversations with Magnus Hestnes on *Sentinella* might go like this...

"Magnus calling Yon, helloo the *Capella Vun*. The *Sentinella* calling the *Capella Vun*, do you pick me up, Yon?"

"Yus Magnus, I pick you up loud and clear and how ver you doing, Magnus?"

"Vell Yon, vee vere not doincc wary good, you know, vee haf a big loomp [it's rough] ya know and our heerings [bait] are so soft and dayy vont stay on dee hooks ya know. And how ver you doincc, Yon?"

"Vell Magnus, vee have nice veder but all vee are getting is dogfisk and skite ya know. But vee vill stay and see vat dee next string has on it."

Three days later…

"Halloo the *Sentinella*, the *Capella Vun* calling *Sentinella*, do you pick me up Magnus?"

"Yus, Yon, I pick you up loud and clear and how ver you doing, Yon?

"Vell, vee are on our vay to the bar [Nahwitti Bar] with a full load."

"Vell, Yesus, Yon, you said you ver yust getting dogfisk and skite."

"Ya, but vee got a few on the last string, ya know."

RALPH SHEMMING CAME TO FRESHWATER BAY IN 1952 ON A troller named *Graydon*. It was a nice boat with a lot of room inside but very little deck space.

Ralph was new at the fishing game but for a newcomer he caught on fast. He was doing good catching pinks and coho but not having much luck with the big springs. At this same time I was catching five to twelve big springs almost every day and this used to get Ralph's goat. He would come and ask me what I was using to catch "the big boys," as he called them, so I told him I was using five-and-a-half Wonders. I told him to watch the tide and to follow me where I went.

He did what I told him and the first day he got two big boys, and after that he would have some big boys every day.

Ralph became a good fisher; he was quick to learn and never made many mistakes. He got to be a top producer of Blackfish

Ralph Shemming on the deck of Graydon *with a couple of the "big boys" around 1949 at Freshwater Bay.* PHOTO COURTESY OF THE SHEMMING FAMILY

Sound. He also got to be good at catching sockeye; he would catch sockeye when no one else was catching any. He sold *Graydon* and bought a real old troller named *S Queen*, and after that he would go north to Milbanke Sound to troll for July and August. On his way home in September he would stop in Blackfish Sound and fish for a while.

CUTHBERT VIVIEN PICKLES first came to Blackfish Sound in 1946 and we all called him "Bert." He'd arrive in June and stay a day or two then go to Blunden Harbour. He'd fish there until mid-August when he would return to fish Blackfish Sound until late September. Bert lived on Denman Island and his boat was *Aye Aye*, which I bought from him in 1951 when I was seventeen, for the sum of $2,200.

Bert travelled alone most of the time but sometimes he would tag along with Gus Linnie. Gus was a red-headed Finlander; his boat had a bright orange cabin that really stood out. I always liked to tease

At Freshwater Bay around 1949. Mr. Pickles always called me a "barnyard savage."
PHOTO BY JAE PROCTOR

Bert and give him a hard time. I don't know why I did this; he just was the kind of guy that inspired that in me. Consequently he always called me a barnyard savage.

Eulogy for Bernard Crowell

WHEN I FIRST MET **BERNARD CROWELL** AROUND 1958 HE HAD a gillnet boat named *Modern Lass*. He was a big Nova Scotian, a rough and ready guy who was a great storyteller and always called a spade a spade. By the time I got to know Bernard better he had a boat named *Tequila*. I had my small troller *Dynamite II* and I only fished in Blackfish Sound. For this reason Bernard would give me a hard time about being scared to get my feet wet—meaning I never went out to the west coast to fish.

Over the years we built up a great friendship. Bernard would come to the mainland to gillnet winter spring salmon and, like me, he trapped in the winter. On his trips to the mainland he always stopped in and spent the evening. It never mattered to Bernard what he was doing, he always loved doing whatever it was he was doing and he always looked at the funny side of everything. He loved to sit and talk about his escapades and some of them were a bit off-colour, but that was the way he was.

In 1971 he bought a 42-foot troller named *Hazel R No. 1* but he changed the name to *Abuptic 2*, the name of a Nova Scotian Indian chief. She was a great sea boat and beautiful as well. When Bernard had *Tequila* he'd begun to troll on weekends when gill-netting was closed and quickly found he liked trolling better, so he'd bought the bigger boat to be able to travel further offshore and stay out longer.

Bernard was sort of a lone wolf out on the fishing grounds. He was never in a group like many of the trollers but always travelled alone. In fact, many of the highliners wouldn't even talk to him. One of the reasons for this was that once in a while he would say on the phone where he was fishing and how many fish he was catching and this was a big no-no to a lot of people. He was not very popular among members of the fleet.

In 1979 when all of the inside waters were closed to trolling I had to go fish the west coast or quit. Out I went and got so seasick I had to go anchor the boat in calm water. I tried all kinds of remedies but nothing worked. One day I went in to Bull Harbour to tie up to the floats and I was so sick I was hoping I would die. A man from a Coast Guard boat came along and asked me what was wrong. When I told him I got seasick he said, "I have some pills that will fix you up." He gave me seven pills and told me, "Take one two hours before you go out."

I did what he said and the next day I was fine, so after that I could fish with the best of them. I was fishing the drop-off by Hope Island and anchoring at Cape Sutil. One day it blew up a northwest gale and I was anchored at Cape Sutil and Bernard was there as well, so I rowed over to visit him.

"Well, how you been doin' fishing, Billy?" he asked me.

"Been doin' good until the last few days, Bernard. It kind of dropped off some."

"Have you gone out to the Yankee Spot?" he asked.

"Nope. I've just been fishing the drop-off and down to Pine Island."

So Bernard got out his chart and showed me how to fish the Yankee Spot and how to use the landmarks to stay on the edge of the bank. He also showed me how I should fish out at the Scott Islands on the west coast and down at Topknot Reef. He told me how deep to fish and what kind of lures to use.

The next day it was a bit rough still so I went to fish over by Pine Island to get out of the swell. About noon Bernard calls me on the phone.

"Well, Billy, how're ya doing?"

"Not very good," I tell him.

"Well get your sorry ass out here to the Yankee Bank and get some fish!"

So I did. Me and my deckhand ran out to the Yankee Bank and we did well. We stayed there and fished the whole season. At first I would run in to Cape Sutil each night and back out again in the morning, which was about an hour and a half run each way. When Bernard found out I was doing all that running he said, "What the hell do you have a hundred fathoms of anchor line for when you go and anchor in four fathoms of water?? For Christ's sake, drop your anchor right on the spot!"

So I did and he was right. I got in more fishing time and also a lot more sleep. Some nights it was a bit rough but I got so I liked it and I fished the Yankee Spot for five full seasons and did well. After those five seasons fishing the Yankee Spot, Bernard said, "Well Billy, it's time you go around to the west coast and try Top Knot." So I did and I liked it there, so that was where I fished for years after that. I also liked fishing the Scott Islands and off Sea Otter Cove.

Bernard never talked to many people on the phone but there were two he talked to every day and they were Tommy Russell on *North Island Star* and Benny Perlini on *Darlene D.* He liked to talk about what he was cooking for dinner or some of the hunting trips he had been on. He would also go on about some of his escapades when he was in the navy. Every morning he'd come on the phone and say, "'Tis a beautiful morning with a gentle breeze and the sun shining off the ripples and I have a bouquet of flowers by my compass and there's the odd fish coming aboard so it's a good day."

The one thing Bernard taught me was to not be afraid of the unknown, which I was when I first went offshore. Bernard would always say, "You can drown ten feet from shore so why worry?"

Bernard liked to hunt deer and geese but he was not a very good shot and was a bit careless with guns. He had the odd hole in the wheelhouse roof of *Abuptic 2* to prove it. His boat was not the cleanest and he hit the beach a time or two and sunk it at least once, but all in all he was a good fisherman and a great friend.

CHAPTER THREE

DOMESTIC HISTORY OF BLACKFISH SOUND

The Nearest Town: Alert Bay

WHEN I WAS A BOY, ALERT BAY WAS OUR LIFELINE AND THE place where all the stores and tradesmen were. It was called "the hub of the North" and was always known as "the Bay." It didn't matter where you were, if you said you were from the Bay everyone just knew you were from Alert Bay. Union Steamships included Alert Bay on their run with the *Cardena* in 1923 and the *Catala* in 1925. In the early '40s cars and taxis came to the village and, after much opposition, the Bay finally gained formal village status in 1946, the year I turned twelve.

Arriving by boat back then, from the east you'd first see the large dairy farm G.H. Skinner started in 1929, and after that four houses that were moved onto shore from the big Powell River camp at the head of Kingcome Inlet. Next was Andy Gibbin's hotel. A small dock was next and above the dock you'd see Al Holman's little store. Parsons Café and Butcher Shop was built on pilings over water and across the road was the Bay Hotel and Café, which was owned by Bill Lawson.

Next was the big Home Oil fuel dock, with fingers going both ways, which was about 150 feet long. The fuel dock was run by a man named Bert Cross. Right at the head of the dock was the

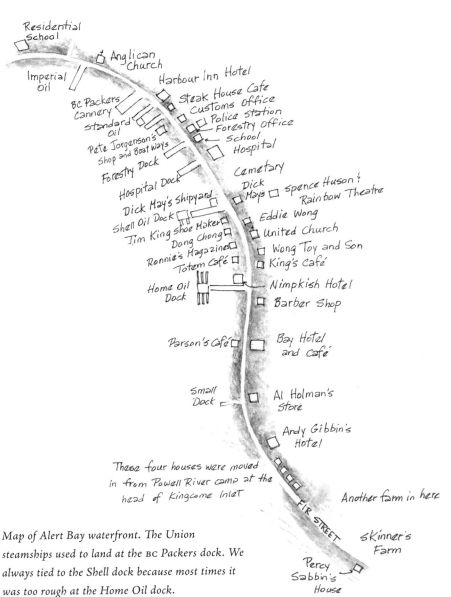

Map of Alert Bay waterfront. The Union
steamships used to land at the BC Packers dock. We
always tied to the Shell dock because most times it
was too rough at the Home Oil dock.

Nimpkish Hotel. This hotel had originally been built on Indian Reserve land in 1920 and it was the oldest hotel in the Bay. In 1925 it had been put on a scow and towed to its spot by the fuel dock. Across the road, Bill Robertson ran the barbershop. I got my first haircut here and cried the whole time. I was so mad my mom made me cut off my long red curls and she was mad at me for crying and called me a sissy.

On the beach side of the road, next, was the Totem Café and across from it was King's Café. Next to King's Café was Wong Toy and Sons Hardware and Dry Goods store and then you'd see the United church and across the road from the church was Ronnie's Magazine Shop beside Dong Chong's store and butcher shop. Beside the church was Eddie Wong's little store and this was a key place for me both as a boy and a young man. When I would go with my dad to Alert Bay he would leave me at Eddie Wong's while he went to the pub and Eddie would give me dishes of soft ice cream while I waited. When I was married to Yvonne, I would leave money with Eddie and we'd come in and tie up at the Shell Oil fuel dock, sometimes quite late, and he would wake up at my knock and give me some of my money. Eddie Wong was a real nice man and always good to me.

An Asian shoemaker named Jim King lived on the beach side of the road and next to that another man named Jim King (not Asian) who ran the Shell Oil fuel dock. Dick May's machine shop and boat ways was next and his house was on the land side of the road, and after that was the graveyard with St. George's Hospital, built in 1909, next to it. The hospital had its own dock, where the big old dock was eventually rebuilt and stands today. Beside the hospital was the school, which finally got indoor plumbing in 1945. In 1955 a new school was built above the village where both

Eddie Wong, he sure was good to me. PHOTO FROM WONG'S MEMORIAL SERVICE

Native and non-Native children were enrolled in Grade 7. On the foreshore, the next dock was the Forestry dock and across the street were the Forestry office, the police station and the Customs office, all in separate buildings.

A café called The Steak House was next and then a tinsmith's shop. On the beach side in front of these was another hardware store, Peterson's Hardware, and Dick Pattinson's Radio Shop and Pete Jorgison's Machine Shop. Dick Bice had opened the Harbour Inn across the road in 1934, the year I was born, and up that road by the inn was the community hall with the bowling alley.

The Standard Oil fuel dock was next and the BC Packers grocery store, (originally operated in the early 1870s by Wesley Spencer and the earliest pioneer, Aulden Huson), the post office and the cannery. A bit further up the bay was the Imperial Oil fuel dock. The Anglican church was across the road and the last building was Ralph Bell's shipyard. So there were plenty of fuel docks and machine shops to service the fishing boats. Right at the very end of the road where it curved was the imposing residential school.

Eventually a water taxi service started up in Alert Bay. The first boat was operated by a man named Charley Hinton with a 30-foot double-ended gillnetter with a two-cylinder Easthope motor. The boat was named *Nemo* and took two hours to go to Freshwater Bay and cost fifteen dollars. A fellow named Barney Williams catered to travelling salesmen and fur buyers and he ran what he called a "jitney" service. His boat *Tranquilla* looked like a small riverboat.

Finally a man named Gill Wood started a real water taxi service with high-speed boats. He had many boats over the years but they were all named *Phantom Lady*. Ray Rosback also operated a water taxi for a few years before he started his Shop-Rite stores business.

Alert Bay was a pretty frightening place for me when I was little but I got to really appreciate it as a young man. Yvonne and I got married in the Pentecostal church in Alert Bay, by the Reverend John Nygaard, and we had a lot of fun in the Bay over the years.

A real important service to residents of the area was the Coast Guard Station based in Alert Bay. You have to understand that everyone had to travel by water and there were hundreds of fishing boats, logging skiffs and small boats for individuals, as well as the mission boats and the steamers to Vancouver. The Coast Guard broadcast the weather and coordinated search and rescue for mariners. Alert Bay Radio had a broadcast schedule to give and receive messages to pass on. They would call every station twice a day, once at 9 a.m. and again at 4:30 in the afternoon. When sending a message you were required to make it as short as possible, which made for some funny messages. A message to Alert Bay Shipyards in the evening, "Yew is ready." Next morning came the answer, "Will pick up yew soon." Another message to a logger who had just come back from a spree down on skid row, or the "lower sections" as he called it: "Darling Daddy, send me one hundred dollars, from Mommy."

To give you a sense of how many people were living in Blackfish Sound and the Broughton Archipelago during the mid-century, I have listed some of the land stations using the government Coast Guard Station frequencies. Every station had a call sign and ours was CJM66. Every station was supposed to reply, although they didn't always.

Acteon Logging Co.: Mackenzie Sound
Atomic Log: Viscount Island
B.C. Forest Products: Gilford Bay
B.C. Forest Products: Glendale Cove
F.H. Benjamin: Kwatsi Bay
W.A. Brown: Indian Pass
J.G. Campbell: Shawl Bay
Charles Creek Logging: Charles Creek
J.B. Collinson: Sullivan Bay
W.B. Crabe: Knight Inlet
A.B. Dick: Village Island
Dot Logging: Lull Bay
Emerson Bay Logging: Greenway Sound
N.A. Erickson: Knight Inlet
Granite Bay Timber: Knight Inlet
J.R.E. Halliday: Kingcome Inlet
I.A. Haslam: Watson Cove
E.J. Hiland: Greenway Sound
Huaskin Logging: Huaskin Lake
Hudson Logging Company: Parson Bay
Jennis Bay Logging: Jennis Bay
Logco Limited: Sim Creek
J. Major: Wells Pass
Mann Logging: Cracroft Island
A.A. McCorkell: Gilford Bay
M.S. Millington: Kingcome Inlet
Minstrel Logging: Glacier Bay
Northern Cedar: Nimmo Bay
Pearse Island Lumber: Pearse Island
F.R. Pederson: Cockatrice Bay

Port McNeill Logging: Cutter Creek
Mrs. Proctor: Freshwater Bay
J.H. Roth: Providence Pass
Scott Logging: Grappler Sound
W.D. Scow: Gilford Reserve
D.E. Smith: Minstrel Island
Sorn Logging: Thompson Sound
Sunrise Logging: Siwash Bay
H. Vasseur: Eden Island
Viner Logging: Moore Bay
H.J. Walden: Baronet Pass
J.M. Wardrop: Echo Bay

The Telegraph Line

WHEN I WAS A BOY, THE TELEGRAPH LINE RAN FROM KELSEY BAY
to the Nimpkish River. In the early '30s the first line was put in
and it just ran along the shore above the high tide line. It hung
from the trees on white porcelain insulators, which you could see
all along the shore.

A few years later a new line was hung about 200 feet inland,
deeper in the bush. This line had brown porcelain insulators that
had "Thomas" on them in raised letters. During World War II
a third line was installed, which consisted of six wires hung on
posts set every 100 feet. Each post had six clear glass insulators.

A "line boat" was stationed at Alert Bay and the crew was on
call 24/7 in case there was a break in the line. The crew had to
travel the length of the line until they found the break. There

First line, second line and third line insulators from the different telegraph lines.
PHOTO BY YVONNE MAXIMCHUK

were stations all along the shore where tie-up lines were laid to run down to the water's edge to make it a bit easier for the crew to land and check the telegraph line.

Typically when the line did break it was due to a bad storm—a tree would blow down across the line. Those days when it was blowing a gale, Mom and I would watch for the line boat, because rather than buck the wind down Johnstone Strait, they'd come into Blackfish Sound and up Baronet Pass, then out Chatham Channel, past the Broken Islands and across the strait. By going this route, if the break was between there and Nimpkish they could just go with the wind, but if it was between there and Kelsey Bay they had to buck the wind to the next station; but at least it was a shorter distance.

I knew one man named Bert Rittenhouse who worked on the line boat for a number of years. It was not a big boat, only about 36 feet long. He told me they sure had some bad trips and that it was a real tough job.

War Time

WHEN THE WAR STARTED I WAS BARELY FIVE, A BIT TOO YOUNG to know what was going on, but my dad was really worried. He spent a lot of time listening to the news. At first it seemed so far away but when the Japanese landed on Attu Island in the Aleutians that brought it closer to home.

The War Department gave us some binoculars and a bunch of forms to fill out. The deal was if we saw some low-flying planes we were supposed to read the numbers on them and write them down and send them in; although we never knew when we might be able to mail them in because we had to rely on sending mail out when a neighbour came by. They also gave us some black fabric to cover our windows at night, which we stuck on the windows with tape. At that time there were so many planes flying over us it was impossible to take the numbers off them all. We were on the main flight path to the Aleutian Islands and some days there was a steady roar of planes overhead. I would look up and see a big V of planes, like geese, anywhere from ten to fifty planes in a V.

When conscription began in Canada, many young men bought fishing boats because if you were a fisherman you would not be called up. The War Department said fishing was necessary to provide food.

Every boat coming up or down the inside waters had to stop at Yorke Island to get clearance. If you did not stop you got a shot across your bow. All boats had to have a big number on their side. These numbers had to be black on white and eight inches high. Most numbers began with YD—ours was YD 7890. Some had a VM before the numbers.

Along with other historic tools in Billy's Museum, the long curled metal item is a fence post from Yorke Island. Rows of barbed wire went through the loops. PHOTO BY YVONNE MAXIMCHUK

The big searchlight at Yorke Island was twelve million candle-power, and we could see the light playing up and down the straits from Freshwater Bay.

AM *Radios*

I CLEARLY REMEMBER THE VERY FIRST AM RADIO WE HAD. IT WAS a De Forrest-Crossley with a big black box three feet long and a foot square. A big speaker sat on top of the box and it took three dry cell batteries to run it, one A battery and two B batteries.

It was our evening ritual to sit and listen to the radio shows: Fred Allen, Eddy Cantor, Will Rogers and Jack Benny. Bob Hope was my favourite, as was *Fibber McGee and Molly*. My dad's favourite was *Lum and Abner* and he really loved the prize fights. Joe Lewis was the heavyweight champion of the world in that era. My mom liked *Death Valley Days* and Art Linkletter's *People Are Funny*. In the morning she just had to listen to Billy Browne's *Breakfast Club*, Will Reeder's *Radio Notebook* and Edward McHugh's *Gospel Hymns and Poems*. She also really liked *The Happy Gang*, *The Whistler* and *Gang Busters*.

Everything had to stop in the evening so we could listen to old Earle Kelly, or, as he was known as, "Mr. Good Evening." He was on CJOR every night at six o'clock with the news, but Mom liked CKWX the best of all the stations.

Around 1940 we got a new radio, a Stewart Warner, and boy, it was a big thing. It stood four feet high and three feet wide. It was a good radio but it was continually blowing tubes. We kept spare tubes on hand at all times but every once in a while we had to wait until Jim Spilsbury came around, which sometimes might be a month or more. We sure missed that radio when we ran out of tubes.

From time to time a man named Bob Richerson would come around in his boat, *Ida T*, but he was no good. One time he took all the tubes out and replaced them; Mom told him it was odd that all the tubes had blown at the same time. Then he wanted to take all the tubes away with him but Mom said, "No way!" The next time Jim Spilsbury came Mom got him to test the old tubes and all but one were still good, and the ones Bob had put in were weak.

In those days when you talked about radios, you always said how many tubes were in it. Ours had seven, which was more powerful than a four-tube. In 1945 I bought a little portable radio which was a four-tube Marconi. By then the A and B batteries were all in one case, called a battery pack, which cost fifteen dollars. I had the Marconi on a little table by my bed and my mom made me turn it off at eight o'clock but I used to take it under the covers where it was too quiet for Mom to hear. I loved to listen to *Tom Mix*, *Red Rider and Little Beaver*, the *Lone Ranger and Tonto*, and *Roy Rogers*.

Mom always wondered why my batteries would go dead so fast. I had a problem of wetting the bed and some nights Mom would wake me up to go pee and one night she caught me with the radio on. I caught hell that night.

I will never forget the day of the first atomic bomb test in Bikini Lagoon. Mom and I sat by the radio for hours listening to see what was going to happen. I was sure the world was going to end—but nothing happened…

Household Items and Making Do

WE HAD A FEW THINGS IN OUR HOUSE TO HELP US COPE WITH everyday life, things that are much improved upon nowadays. We had a davenport couch that could be folded down and made into a double bed. Some people called this a "Winnipeg Couch."

Everyone had a wood heater and ours was a "circulator" with the name Good Cheer and it worked very well. Our cook stove was a National and it burnt stove oil. It had a wick burner called a "silent glow" and it burnt well with a pretty blue flame. The oil stove needed a tank and the tank held only two gallons, so it had to be filled every single morning. I have never seen another one like it. It sat upside down on a green enamel bowl with stainless steel legs, and there was a spring in the cap of the tank. As the stove burnt oil, the tank would gurgle as air filled the emptying space and let oil in to refill the stand.

Mom got this stove and tank in 1934, the year I was born, and she used it until 1983. In later years, either my wife or I filled the tank for her. Gawd, how I hated that tank.

Mom's old cookstove with the oil container which I had to fill every single morning. PHOTO BY JAE PROCTOR

For lights, we had coal oil lamps and it seemed like we were always trimming the wicks. The flame would get pointed and soot up the chimney. I would fiddle with it until I had the wick cut just right, turn it up for a brighter light and the wick would not roll up evenly. The best burners were White Star but they were hard to get. Mom was always cursing the burners until she broke down and bought an Aladdin lamp. It gave off a bright light but the mantle was very fragile and would break easily, so after a short time it was back to the old lamps.

Then Mom got a coal oil lantern, much like a Coleman gas lantern, except it burnt coal oil. This lantern had two mantles and a little cup we had to put alcohol in to preheat it. Sometimes when we put the match to it, it would flare up. Mom hated this lamp, too. When it did light it made a loud fuzzing noise. One night when I went to light the thing, it blazed up and I grabbed it and threw it

Good Cheer heaters. FROM THE MARSHALL WELLS CATALOGUE

"Good Cheer" **Wood Circulating Heaters**

MODEL 24-27

DEVELOPED TO GIVE CLEAN, HEALTHFUL, MOIST WARM AIR, JUST LIKE A PIPELESS FURNACE, ASSURING GENEROUS WARMTH IN COLDEST WEATHER.

Full open grill top allows an easy flow of air through the heater, adding tremendously to its efficiency. Heating capacity is greater than many basement furnaces, due to no loss through pipes. Every heat unit is radiated from the large grill top mica front and circulating sections. Large end feed door, 11½ inches wide by 13 inches high, is a great convenience and permits the handling of large blocks of wood.

Height, 38 inches; outside casing, 20 x 27 inches; mica doors, 13 x 13 inches; ash pit and firebox, 14 x 24 x 27 inches high; grate surface, 14 x 24 inches. Weight, 290 lbs.

No. 24—27B—Grained Walnut Porcelain Enamel, Nickel-Plated Trim.
Each $72.00
No. 24-27A—Polished Blued Steel, Nickel Plated Trim.
Each $60.00

No. 24-27A

"Good Cheer"
**Open Grate
Heaters**

Get the Most for Your
Heating Dollars

out and burnt my hand badly. So that was the end of the "fuzzer" as Mom called it.

We had no running water at our house in Freshwater Bay, just a tap out in the woodshed attached to a 400-foot line that came from the creek. We had no hot water tank either so all water had to be heated on the stove. We had a Jubilee washing machine. This contraption had a big wooden tub with a lid on it and a fly wheel. It had a long wooden handle that you pushed back and forth. There was a wringer on the side that had to be cranked as you put the clothes through. As soon as I got old enough, when I was about twelve, it became my job to do the washing.

Most of the time Mom would do all the washing by hand with the washboard because it took so long to heat the water for the machine; if I got my clothes really dirty then she would make me wash them in the machine. Mom used to iron everything. She always had sad irons on the back of the stove and she also had a Coleman gas iron, which burnt naphtha gas. This contraption also had a tendency to flare up and Mom would curse it. The thing was always either too hot or too cold.

Our floors were covered with Congoleum, which was nice and easy to keep clean. Three rooms were wallpapered but my bedroom had kalsomine on the walls. Mom put on a new coat every couple of years. On our kitchen table Mom had oilcloth. There were lots of colours to choose from. Ours was always blue with a flower design on it. We had no refrigerator, just a cooler out in the woods Mom called a "meat safe."

Of course there was no inside bathroom. We had an outhouse that was 100 feet away and used to stink like hell. It was a two-holer: one big hole and a smaller one for me. We used to put chloride of lime down to kill the smell but it didn't help much.

Down in the basement Dad had a workshop with some interesting old tools. I still have some of them. His pride and joy was his grindstone. This was mounted on a bench that you could sit on, with a foot pedal you worked to turn the grindstone. Dad used it to sharpen axes. One day I got hold of a can of aluminum paint and I went on a painting binge and painted everything I could see including the grindstone. I sure got hell for that. Dad made me clean it all off, which turned out to not be easy. The paint had soaked into the porous stone, so to clean it, I had to hold a file against the stone and turn it with the foot pedal. It took me hours. I learned not to paint a grindstone.

When I was about fourteen, six years after my dad died, I decided I would make some lead sinkers. I had watched my dad do it many times so I figured it was no big deal. I had Dad's big pot that he would melt the lead in and heated up about 15 pounds of lead in the pot. I had an old 10-pound lead, so I decided I would add that to the mix. I dropped the cold weight into the hot lead. I soon found out that was a no-no. The lead began to bubble and then it exploded. The hot lead blew out of the pot and some stuck to the ceiling, some landed on my head and some ran down inside my gumboots and burnt my feet.

Years later, I found out what takes place when you pour lead into a mould. Sometimes it ends up with a hole in the centre of the lead, and from this hole there will be a small vent. When you use the lead, water gets into the hole in the centre. Through use, the lead gets bumped around and the vent seals up. So now you have a lead with a hole in the centre that is full of water. When I put the lead in the pot of molten lead, the water in the centre of the hole boiled and presto!—I had a bomb.

My Mom's Superstitions

MY MOTHER WAS A VERY SUPERSTITIOUS PERSON, PARTICULAR-ly around Christmas and New Year's. If she was decorating a Christmas tree and it happened to fall over she would have to throw it out and go find another one. On New Year's Eve she burned a candle in the window so the new year could find its way in, and now I always do this, too. New Year's Day I always had to wear something new or else I would be wearing rags all year. When she made a New Year's Day visit she would roll a can of food in the door ahead of her, which meant you would have food all year. I do this at Al and Yvonne's every year with a can of evaporated milk. If you had a wood stove my mom would bring a stick of wood from her pile and put it in your stove; this meant you would be warm all year.

My mom said it was bad luck to watch a boat go out of sight or start anything on a Friday. I never start a voyage on a Friday; many fishermen believe the same and will delay a trip if it means leaving the dock on a Friday. Also like fishermen, she never opened a can upside down. And she always had to go out of a house by the same door she came in. Green was a colour she never wore; she said if you wear green, you will wear black. Numbers five and nine were very bad luck. If there were five people at the dinner table she always set a plate to make six.

Sunday, June 23, 1946, there was a big earthquake. Mom was sewing and I was down in the basement. When the earthquake hit she thought I was doing something that was shaking the house. She yelled at me to stop and I ran upstairs and the old house was shaking so bad that the goldfish bowl was half emptied. After that Mom would never sew on a Sunday.

Shaving

I KNEW A LOT OF FISHERMEN AS I WAS GROWING UP AND SOME of them helped me learn about fishing and some of them I helped in turn. There were other things happening for me besides fishing and I can remember when I thought I needed to start shaving. Ralph Shemming gave me a razor—a haywire contraption called a Rolls Razor, in a silver case about eight inches long by three inches wide with a lid on each side.

A hone lay on one side and on the other side, a leather strop. You could sharpen the damn thing like this: when you opened the lid you took the handle of the razor and pushed it back and forth, and as you did this the razor would flip over and back so it would sharpen both sides. Well it was supposed to sharpen both sides but it never seemed to get sharp.

Outboard Motors I Have Owned

IN 1947 I BOUGHT A 2 HP JOHNSON. IT WAS A GOOD LITTLE motor and it sure beat rowing. I had it mounted on a 12-foot flat-bottomed skiff and used it for many years, mainly to troll commercially. It had a little gas tank on the top that only held about a pint of gas and I was able to fill it while I was trolling, without shutting the motor off.

This motor had two cylinders and sometimes it misfired a lot, which made it difficult to hold my speed. I took the wire off one of the two spark plugs and found it ran well on only one cylinder. One day I was filling the tank with gas and the wire that was off the spark plug was sparking and the gas tank caught on fire. A flame four feet high shot out of the tank and the gas can caught on fire, too, so I threw the can overboard and threw my coat over the motor. The fire went out and I was back fishing in no time.

My next motor was a 16 hp Scott-Atwater on the 14-foot *Gee Whiz*. It turned out to be a piece of junk and I did a lot of paddling home. I loaned it to my brother-in-law one day; he wanted to go to Alert Bay. He went to the bar and had a few with the boys and when he went to fuel up, Jim King at the fuel dock said, "You need to put oil in the gas."

To which John replied, "Oh no, this motor don't use oil in the gas." Jim knew this was wrong because I had fuelled up there many times. Anyway, John got towed home that night.

"What happened to my motor?" I said.

"Oh," he says, "it started to miss, then it just stopped." So I went and gave the starting rope a pull and discovered the motor was seized, so

I found this motor upstairs in Ray Rosback's Shop-Rite Marine store in Port McNeill, it's the same as his old Johnson Sea Horse except it is in mint condition. PHOTO BY YVONNE MAXIMCHUK

that was the end of that motor. I did buy another Scott-Atwater because I would have spare parts off the old one, and I used it for two years.

I went up Wakeman Sound duck hunting with Bud Brown and Bobby Halliday and had that boat and motor with me. While I was there it came up a storm, so I took the motor off and put it down the hatch so it wouldn't get wet. It was the first time I had been to Wakeman Sound so I didn't really know where to go, but Bud and Bobby said we should go to Charles Creek, which we did. But by the time we got there, *Gee Whiz* was gone. I went to look for it the next morning but never found it so I was sure it had sunk. I heard later it was found nearby Hopetown Village the day after I lost it. That boat was seen running around for years and the last time I saw it, it was lying on the bank of the Kingcome River by the village.

My next boat was a 12-foot round-bottom moulded birch boat with a 9.5 Evinrude. The motor was good but the boat was no good, it just fell apart. After that I built a 16-foot scow, which I used for clam digging. I had a 7 hp West Bend outboard on it. My wife and I got a lot of use out of that little motor but one day we went out fishing on *Fisher Boy* with the scow tied alongside. I turned too sharp on the way home and the scow rolled over and went into the propeller, which cut the scow in half. So I had to build a new scow.

About this time I was trapping in Wakeman and all I was using was a small rowboat I had built. I was doing a lot of rowing so I bought a 4 hp Chrysler outboard. When I was rowing I had always been warm but with the outboard I was always cold, except when I was cranking the damn thing. Every time I went ashore to check a trap I would have to crank for ten minutes to get it going. So one day I was crossing Wakeman and when I was halfway across I stopped and unbolted the motor and dropped it overboard. When it was lying in 1,400 feet of water I went back to rowing and was warm again.

Gordon Halliday gave me an old 16-foot fibreglass speedboat that was a haywire piece of junk. Its windshield had come off a truck. I patched it up and painted it bright pink with blue trim and called it *Pink Dink*. I bought a 40 hp Evinrude for it. This motor had a bad habit of breaking drive shafts so we did a lot of paddling in that boat, too, but I was always lucky: it always broke down close to home. It was a heavy old boat but we used it for a few years.

In 1971 I went to Howe Sound to the Sun Salmon Derby to see if I could win a new boat. There were about four hundred boats in the water but I had the only pink one. I didn't win but it was fun. After a couple of years I bought another 40 hp Evinrude to put on it. Then one night a real bad southwest storm hit and it did a lot of damage to *Pink Dink* so I sold it to a Native guy for twenty-five dollars and he ran around with it for a while until it ended up on the riverbank in Kingcome Inlet.

In the '70s Ray Rosback was building Surfers in Alert Bay, a sturdy speedboat style that seemed to be everything I needed in a boat. He had them in 16-, 19-, 21-, and 24-foot lengths and I bought a 16-foot Surfer, which came with a 60 hp Evinrude. Boy, I was in seventh heaven with a new motor and a new boat, but the motor was not that good and only lasted about a year and a half. I bought another one and it was the same. I went through six 60 hp Evinrudes and one 70 horse, which lasted about six hours. I was at the sea lion rock at the end of Fife Sound and it just seized up solid. I paddled into Joe Cove to Bobby Lamont's camp and a yacht tied up there towed me home. That was the last straw; I stopped buying Evinrude outboard motors.

The motor I bought next was a 50 hp Classic 50 Mercury, which was by far the best motor I had had up to that time. I ran it for over three years and it finally just wore out from use. I bought a new 50 hp Mercury but it was not as good as the old Classic 50. I used that one for two years and then I bought a 60 hp Mariner, a Japanese version of Mercury. It turned out to be a piece of junk but then I sunk the Surfer so that was the end of the Mariner.

The old Surfer was a bit beat up after that so I gave it to Bobby Lamont and bought a new one from Ray. I bought a 60 hp Yamaha Enduro motor, a two-stroke, and it was the best motor I had ever had. I went through three 60 horse Yamaha Enduros, running about 2,500 hours on each before I bought a new one. Yamaha went to four-stroke motors, which are not as polluting because the oil is not burned with the gas but just stays in the motor and lubricates it. The four-stroke Yamaha has been the best motor by far and I have had five 60 hps over the years. Now I have three 16-foot Surfers, two with 60 hp Yamahas and one with a 70 hp Yamaha. I use two of these boats for log salvaging and one of them to go to Port McNeill and go touring and fishing in. When I am log salvaging I put on 1,500 hours a year, which is a lot of hours for an outboard motor. The development of better and more reliable motors has sure made my life easier the last twenty-five years, not so much paddling at inconvenient moments.

Marine Gas Engines

WHEN I WAS A BOY THERE WERE
many makes and models of gas engines. The most popular was the
Easthope, which a lot of people
called a "Lasthope." They were
available in many horsepowers,
from as small as a four up to sixty.
There were four, five, six, seven and
eight horsepower Easthopes and
the ones I saw most often were four
and seven. The others you didn't
see too many of. These were all
one-cylinder engines—or "one-lun-
gers"—as most people called them.
When they were running they went
putt putt putt.

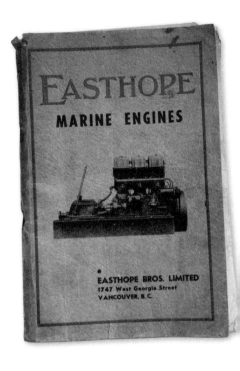

*Easthope Bros. motor plate. If you google the serial number of any Easthope
Motor you will find the original owner of record.* PHOTO BY YVONNE MAXIMCHUK

Easthope also had two-, three- and four-cylinder models and the most popular was the 10–14 hp; when it was running it went *two bits two bits two bits.*

The most popular of the three-cylinder models was the 15–18 hp and when one was running the sound it made was *cup of tea cup of tea cup of tea.* I only ever saw one four-cylinder Easthope.

After Easthope, the next most popular engine was the Palmer, which came in one- and two-cylinder models. Mostly I would see the one-cylinder six-horse. Palmers came in two types; one was the L head, the other was the T head. The L head had both the intake and exhaust valves on one side of the head. The T head had the intake valve on one side of the head and the exhaust valve on the other. I only ever saw two of the two-cylinder Palmer.

Kedge anchor. PHOTO BY
YVONNE MAXIMCHUK

Anchors Aweigh

AN ANCHOR IS A VERY IMPORTANT piece of equipment on every boat or ship. Ever since mankind took to the sea anchors have been around; they appear in the symbolism of many civilizations as an emblem of hope. Anchors were known to all nations, even in ancient times.

First, let us consider the "old-fashioned" anchor, as some call it. I know it as the kedge or halibut anchor, or mud hook. This anchor was de-

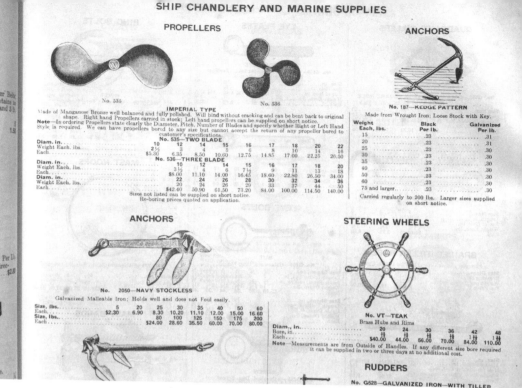

PROPELLERS

No. 535   No. 536

IMPERIAL TYPE

Made of Manganese Bronze well balanced and fully polished. Will bind without cracking and can be bent back to original shape. Right hand Propellers carried in stock; Left hand propellers can be supplied on short notice.

Note—In ordering Propellers state clearly the Diameter, Pitch, Number of Blades and specify whether Right or Left Hand Style is required. We can have propellers bored to any size but cannot accept the return of any propeller bored to customer's specifications.

No. 535—TWO BLADE

Diam. in.	10	12	14	15	16	17	18	20	22
Weight Each, lbs.	2½	4	5	6	8	10	14	16	
Each	$5.30	6.35	8.50	10.60	12.75	14.85	17.00	22.25	26.50

No. 536—THREE BLADE

Diam. in.	10	12	14	15	16	17	18	20
Weight Each, lbs.		3½	4	6	7½	9	11	13	18
Each	$8.00	11.10	14.00	16.44	18.60	22.80	26.50	34.00
Diam. in.	22	24	26	28	30	32	34	36
Weight Each, lbs.	20	24	26	29	33	37	44	50
Each	$42.40	50.90	61.50	73.20	84.00	100.00	114.50	140.00

Sizes not listed can be supplied on short notice.
Re-boring prices quoted on application.

ANCHORS

No. 187—KEDGE PATTERN

Made from Wrought Iron; Loose Stock with Key.

Weight Each, lbs.	Black Per lb.	Galvanized Per lb.
15	.23	.31
20	.23	.31
25	.23	.30
30	.23	.30
35	.23	.30
40	.23	.30
50	.23	.30
60	.23	.30
75 and larger	.23	.30

Carried regularly to 200 lbs. Larger sizes supplied on short notice.

ANCHORS

No. 2050—NAVY STOCKLESS

Galvanized Malleable Iron; Holds well and does not Foul easily.

Size, lbs.	5	20	25	30	35	40	50	60
Each	$2.30	6.90	8.30	10.20	11.10	12.00	15.00	16.60
Size, lbs.			80	100	125	150	175	200
Each		$24.00	28.60	35.50	60.00	70.00	80.00

STEERING WHEELS

No. VT—TEAK

Brass Hubs and Rims

Diam., in.	20	24	30	36	42	48
Bore, in.	1⅛	1⅛	1⅛	1⅛	1¼	1¼
Each	$40.00	44.00	56.00	70.00	84.00	110.00

Note—Measurements are from Outside of Handles. If any different size bore required it can be supplied in two or three days at no additional cost.

RUDDERS

No. G528—GALVANIZED IRON—WITH TILLER

Marshall-Wells Company anchors. PHOTO BY YVONNE MAXIMCHUK

veloped after centuries of trial and experiment as the best form for quick grip on the ocean floor and sturdy holding quality. This form of the anchor is very old. Coins found in the catacombs of Rome show anchors essentially the same in form. Even before anchors were made of metal, the same general form of anchor was made of wood. These were made to sink by lashing rocks to the shank.

Kedge anchors are not used much by boaters today because they are hard to stow because of the stock. But all longline and halibut fishermen still use the kedge (halibut) anchor. The newer stockless anchors are the top choice today mainly because they are easy to stow and fit nicely in a bow roller.

Today there are many types of anchors and everyone has his favourite. One older type is the navy anchor. It is used by a lot of big ships because it has no stock and fits well in the hawse pipe in the bow of a ship. The navy anchor is almost as old as the kedge.

The Babbitt anchor is my favourite. It holds well in most bottoms and doesn't foul or tangle up. That's what I have on *Ocean Dawn*. The Northill is a good anchor but is bad for fouling. Another one that is bad for fouling is the Danforth, which also doesn't stow well but does have good holding quality. The Forfjord is like a Babbitt but with a shorter shank, and it stows well and has good holding quality. Another anchor called the Davis Sea Hook is just like the Forfjord. The "plow" anchor—it pretty much looks like a plow—is a very popular anchor among the yachters. One way or another every boater needs an anchor.

Things We Don't Use Anymore

mendets: These were tiny nuts with a bolt and two washers and two cork gaskets. We used them to mend holes in enamel pots.

gimlet (pictured): A handy little auger used to drill small holes to put in small nails or screws.

coping saw: Used for cutting circles and odd shapes.

cross-cut saw: Used before chainsaws
    became common.
spoke shave: This was used to make the wooden
    spokes for buggy wheels.
blindman's rule: Two-foot-long four-fold ruler
hand drill or hand breast drillhand
boom augers: For boring four-inch holes in the ends
    of boomsticks.
shoe last: My dad had one of these, used as a form
    to hold a boot or shoe so you could put nails
    on a new sole or heel. A lot of fishermen would
    come and use Dad's shoe last to nail on a new
    "half-sole."
mucilage: Clear glue. The bottle had a little rubber
    top and it was easy to spread and I used it to
    stick papers and things in my scrapbook.
wind-up alarm clock camera: The kind for which
    you wound the film roll every time you took a
    picture, and there were only eight pictures to a
    roll of film.
gramophone: Or phonograph; ours was called His
    Master's Voice. The old records were 78 rpm. I
    had to crank it up to play one record and change
    the needle after playing four.
Petter diesel power plant: When Dad was alive, we
    had this two-cylinder power plant called a Petter
    Hot Head. It had two blowtorches mounted on
    the side, one for each cylinder head. The flame
    from the torches went in a little hood on the
    head to direct the flame down into the head. Dad

lit the torches and let them run about fifteen minutes, then he would turn a big crank to get the thing going. It had two big fly wheels and when it started it was really noisy. Mom hated that thing, and all we had that used electricity was one small light in each room. It wasn't worth it to her. After dad drowned, Mom could not start it, so she sold it.

Our Animals

MY DAD GOT A COW FROM THE HALLIDAYS IN KINGCOME INLET. They brought her in on their boat and kicked her overboard and she swam ashore. She had a calf about a month later; I loved that little calf and spent a lot of time in the barn with it. Mom and I did not like the milk from the cow. Dad used to try to make me drink it but I thought it tasted like the cow smelled, so after a while he gave up. I think it was because I was raised on canned Carnation milk. I still don't like milk any other way but out of a can. After Dad was gone neither Mom nor I milked the cow and she got all swelled up and ran around mooing. The next time Mr. and Mrs. Kimball came around they took the calf and Bob Davis took the cow away on a float.

Another animal Dad brought home was a goat. He went down to Beware Pass and brought back one of the goats that were living on Klaoitsis Island in front of Karlukwees (Ka Lugwis) Village. Two days after he brought the goat home it died; Mom said it died because it was lonely.

When I was small we had mallard and Pekin ducks and geese. I remember we gave the geese away but kept the ducks. I loved the ducks. We had a big pond in the creek and a little shed for them, but the eagles got most of them, unfortunately. We were down to six mallards and one night Mom told me to go shut in the ducks because she heard them making noise the night before. She thought a mink was after them, so I went and locked the door. The next morning when I went to let them out, all the ducks were dead. The mink had chewed a hole in the floor and killed them all. If I had not locked them in they could have got away.

Years later someone gave us six mallards and they were a bit wild but we fed them and they got to be tame, until one day we had a bad storm and the ducks all flew away. We never saw them for many months. One day in the spring Mom and Dad had a big bonfire on the beach and two mallard hens came flying in. One of them walked right up to the fire and fell down dead and the other one flew away. It was real odd.

Tax Men and Salesmen

EVEN THOUGH WE LIVED FAR FROM THE CITY, PAYING TAXES ON our earnings was still something that had to be done every year. Many people had no education and relied on different fellows who came around to help them do their taxes. One man who came around every year in his boat *Van-Dee* was named Tom Feely. He would go to all the little camps and do people's income tax returns. Tom always wore a blue suit and tie, but his pants were dirty and shiny with wear. He took his meals in the cookhouses at the logging camps. The longer it took him to do the taxes, the more free meals he could cadge. He got to be such a mooch that a lot of the camps would not let him tie up. As he got older he made many mistakes so he was not getting much business. He finally sold his boat to a Native man who changed the name to *Ga Gun Too*.

Another tax man worked out of Minstrel Island; he went by the name of B.L. Cope and Sons. His boat was named *Rover*, and he never came unless you contacted him first.

There were also a lot of travelling salesmen that used to come around. One fellow that came to our camp in the fishing season was Jim Whitehead on *Jolly Jumbo*. Jim sold all kinds of stuff like costume jewellery and clothing. He also had three "hairdressers" on board, or so they were called. Once in a while Mom would go on board and buy a pair of slippers or some other item she needed. Another salesman I loved to see come in was George Bradshaw on *Adventus*. George sold all the new fishing tackle. Most of it was useless but I was a sucker for new gear and he knew it. He travelled for Gundry Bilmac, which was a big commercial and marine supplier.

Then there was Alex Sohonavich on *Coastliner*, who sold all kinds of junk, mostly jewellery and clothing. One day while he was at our camp he got a line in his propeller and I helped him get it out. He gave me a cigarette lighter.

Not all the salesmen were visitors you would want. One day in mid-winter a boat came in and the man came up to the house.

"I am Mr. Swanson and I need some stove oil and I need some bread and eggs," he informed Mom.

"I have none to spare, I'm sorry," said Mom. Mr. Swanson got quite upset and told Mom she should let him have what he wanted. Mom tried to explain to him that she had no way to get these things, that she had to rely on someone going by to get what she needed and never knew when that might be.

We found out later the fellow was a preacher and really was just a bum. At the time there was a logging camp in Parson Bay that was owned by Gus Swanberg. This Mr. Swanson had gone to his camp after he left ours and Gus had invited him in. He started to tell Gus how Mrs. Proctor would not give him what he wanted.

"You mean to say you were trying to bum from a widow?!"

Mr. Swanson replied that he needed a few things and at this, Gus picked him up and threw him on his boat and turned the boat loose.

"And don't you never come back here!"

The Story of My Old House

THERE ONCE WAS A HOUSE BUILT IN BOND SOUND BY JIMMY Moffat, a logger who logged along the shore of the sound with an A-frame. The house had a T-shaped roof and a simple front wall with a door and two windows. He likely got the lumber for the framing, fir, from Walden's mill and it was lined with cedar V-joint, which came in bundles from Vancouver. It had a little kitchen, a little wee bathroom, two bedrooms and a combined living/dining room.

Ted Brooks was a forestry officer and he bought the float-house from Jimmy and had it moved into Echo Bay. Ted sold it to Harold Bachen, who ran a fish packer named *Ballerina No. 1* for gillnet fish. In 1958 I bought it for $3,800 and towed it to Insect Island. For the next three years I towed the floathouse

Here's my old house tied up by my property on Gilford Island. My mom's house is to the left, and just above her house you can just see the house Patty and I built on the land. PHOTO BY JAE PROCTOR

from Insect Island to Yokohama Bay, back to Baker Island, then back down to Yokohama Bay to run the fish camp. I moved it to my bay around the corner from Echo Bay in December of 1961 and we moved ashore in 1982, after I'd bought the land from Mark Millington and built my house. My daughter Joanie and

her husband Phil lived in the floathouse while they were building their house through 1983.

Over the years I'd rebuilt the house and added an upstairs and I
also put a new float underneath. I sold the house in 1983 for $4,500
to Bill McLeod, after he came to get the hatchery started up. I
towed it to Scott Cove, where he and Frances lived in it for four
years. Bill rebuilt the whole inside with photofinish wallboard and
nice trim and he sold it to Dave Tarkanen, for the astonishing price
of $75,000. Dave towed it to Shawl Bay and lived there with Edna
Brown for four or five years. I think it was one of the few houses I
know of that got sold for more rather than less each time it got a
new owner.

The next owner was a man from Sullivan Bay, who lived in it a
short time but by then the float was sinking pretty bad and rather
than repair or replace it, he burnt up the house. So that was the
end of the house that had been our home for twenty-four years.

The Canadian Hydrographic Survey

THE MAKING OF NEW CHARTS FOR THE BRITISH COLUMBIA COAST
began in 1951 and was a big project. The Department of Mines
and Resources owned the two boats used for this work. One was
named *Parry* and the bigger one, the 100-foot-long *Wm. J. Stewart*,
worked around Blackfish Sound and the Broughton Archipelago.
Along with the big boat were six smaller open boats, each about
24 to 26 feet long; these boats were quite wide and I do not know
what kind of motors were in them. The *Wm. J. Stewart* anchored
in Freshwater Bay sometimes and also at Farewell Harbour and

Sunday Harbour. After they were anchored, each day two or three men would climb in each of the smaller boats and they would all go their separate ways.

The procedure was to create a grid on a chart that would be the platform on which an exact location of rocks and various depths could be plotted in order to map the undersea bottom. Each boatful of men would run to a spot where they would build a little stone marker that could hold a stake; it had to be a spot that could be seen for a long way. Then the men would run the boat back and forth plotting a grid. They placed small stone cairns all over the area and sometimes they simply painted a rock with white paint as a mark. If some of the cairns to mark grid points were a long distance apart the crew painted on rocks in between in order to keep the line straight. It would take them two or three

The hydrographic marine charts used by mariners today were created using grid lines that marked places to survey depths. Here's an overview of how the grid lines would have been laid out at Freshwater Bay.

days to lay out the grid in each area. If I remember correctly, each grid line was about four feet from the next.

Once they had an area mapped out in a grid the men would travel along the line taking soundings at regular intervals. Because of the grid they were able to take a huge number of soundings and plot a precise chart of what was below the surface. This work took up to two years I believe and the resulting charts are the hydrographic marine charts still used by mariners today.

This is how the grid lines would have looked in Queen Charlotte Strait near Fife Sound.

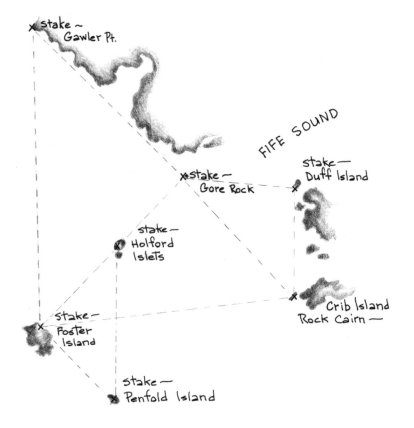

This big rock was painted white to use as a marker, and there is a direct line of sight to Spout Island, another point of reference. PHOTO BY YVONNE MAXIMCHUK

CHAPTER FOUR
BILLY'S LIFE STORIES

Auxiliary Coast Guard

I HAVE BEEN A MEMBER OF THE AUXILIARY COAST GUARD FOR over forty years. I signed up in 1973 when I got *Twilight Rock* built. What this means is I am supposed to stand by on Channel 16 on the VHF radiophone 24/7, which I do when I am on the boat or in the house.

One evening in August 1959, long before I joined the Auxiliary Coast Guard, when all the other trollers were in for the night, a troller called *Tyrone* hit a rock off Bold Head. The crew saw the boat was going to sink so they ran it up on the beach at Bold Head and climbed off. They were a couple of greenhorns, a man and his grandson; the grandfather was over sixty years old. The two decided to walk to our camp, which was a mile and a half through thick salal bush. This would be a tough hike in the daylight but I would not want to do it in the dark. Our camp was in Yokohama Bay and my house was on a float.

The two got to the house at 1 a.m. and woke me up by throwing rocks from the shore. I got up to see what was going on, brought them into the house and they told me the story.

"What about the boat?" I asked.

"We'll get it when it gets daylight," they replied. But it was blowing a bit of westerly and I knew there would be a swell on Bold Head. So I got dressed and got my boat going. I needed someone to come with me to put a line on the *Tyrone* to tow it in so I woke my friend Bob Palmer, got my rowboat tied up to *Dynamite II* and we were away. There was a fair swell rolling in when we got to Bold Head so I nosed in as close as I dared and Bob climbed into the rowboat and got to shore.

The fishing boat was upside down on the shore and the only place to tie a rope to was the propeller shaft so that's where he tied it. It was hard towing that boat upside down and if I speeded up the boat would dive so I had to go real slow. It took two hours to go the mile and a half but we finally got it tied up in front of my house.

The boat sat close to shore in fairly shallow water and in the morning at low tide the mast was stuck in the bottom and pushed the boat up out of the water; so the boat sat, stuck on its mast, upside down. It was easy to see where the damage was and the man and his grandson put a patch on it. At high tide the big packer came in, and they wrapped a line around the boat and rolled it right side up. The two fishermen pumped it out and were back out fishing the next day.

Another time, during a gillnet opening in August about 1977, I was running from Cape Scott to Pine Island in a big swell. It was blowing about ten knots southeast and I saw what looked like a big log on the horizon. I took a look through the binoculars and saw it was a person in a small boat so I ran out to him and helped him on board. It was a sixteen-year-old boy and he was the deckhand on a gillnet boat and the boat's battery had died. The skipper had sent his young deckhand to paddle to Bull Harbour for help and when I picked him up he still had six miles to go. The boat was a six-foot Sportyak and the boy

Tyrone *being rolled right side up by the packer* Melvin E *after the bottom was patched.* PHOTO BY YVONNE PROCTOR

had only one oar. What with the swell and the little chop on the surface from the southeast wind he'd had to stop often to bail.

We ran out and found the gillnetter. I took one of my batteries out of my engine room and we got it on the deck. We both had to pull up one of our stabilizer poles so we could get alongside each other. This is not an easy matter in a swell but we got the battery onto his boat and I stood by until he got going. The skipper and his young deckhand went on their way and they left my battery in Port Hardy, where I picked it up later in the season.

ONE AUGUST DAY IN 1989, MY DAUGHTER JOANIE AND I WERE trolling at Top Knot and it came up a gale of southeast so we ran into San Josef Bay. The next day it was still blowing storm force, 70 knots, so no one went out fishing. There were about forty boats anchored in San Josef Bay. The day before, a small troller had rolled over off Top Knot when it took a wave over the stern, and the fisherman and his girlfriends had got into a small Sportyak and been picked up by another troller. The boat was vulnerable to scavenging and I hated to see the young fellow who owned it lose his shirt.

In the morning we could see the upside-down boat out in the mouth of the bay. It was drifting toward the islands outside Sea Otter Cove and I knew if it hit those islands it would smash up for sure.

"I'm gonna try and get a line on that boat and tow it into Sea Otter," I told Joanie.

"No way am I coming!" said Joanie, so I dropped her off on John Gibson's boat and took John and Dave Gark along. Dave had a small Zodiac so we were able to get close to the rolled-over boat. There was a good big swell so I got my boat between the incoming waves and broke the swell a bit so Dave could get a line around the propeller shaft. It took us a couple of hours to tow because the poles were dragging on the bottom as we got into Sea Otter Cove, then we tied it up to a little island.

I phoned the Coast Guard at Alert Bay to let them know that the boat was recovered and Alert Bay phoned the Coast Guard in Bull Harbour. They sent their boat, *Cape Sutil*, around to Sea Otter in the teeth of the gale, to mark the fishing boat. It took them six hours bucking into the gale to come around the top end of Vancouver Island. They went into Sea Otter and drove in a steel rod with a flag on it to mark the boat, and went back to Bull Harbour.

I knew the owner of the boat lived in Port Hardy so I phoned him and told him where the boat was. When the wind went down he came around in his seine boat and rolled the troller right side up, pumped it out and towed it back to Port Hardy. I went to take a look and the only damage done was where the Coast Guard had driven in the steel rod and split the varnished guard rail. Nothing was missing off the boat except for one cannonball.

ONCE I TOWED TWO TROLLERS FROM SEA OTTER COVE TO PORT Hardy. It is not easy off Cape Scott if there is a swell, which there is most of the time. Then you have to catch the right tide to go over Nahwitti Bar because the swell is very bad on an ebb tide.

One morning I was running through Christie Pass, also known as God's Pocket, when a man came on the radio with a mayday. So I gave him a call and he said he'd hit a rock in Christie Pass.

"I am in Christie Pass and I don't see any boat," I said.

"Oh, I'm in God's Pocket," he says. "I am right in God's Pocket." I look around but I still don't see any boat. Right about then another man comes on the radio and says he can see a boat on the rocks.

"It's in Harlequin Bay," he says. Harlequin Bay is on the other end of Hurst Island from Christie Pass. So I ran around to Harlequin Bay and there he was, sitting high and dry. I anchored and rowed over.

"How the hell did you get up there?" I asked him. He still thought he was in God's Pocket. I have no idea how he got there because he had to go through a pass that was a lot narrower than Christie Pass. Anyway, the tide was still ebbing for another three hours and his boat would not float until about six the next morning, so I stayed anchored for the night.

In the morning as the tide was coming in there was a bit of a swell with it from the sound. As the boat began to float it started to pound a bit against the rocks so I tied a line from my boat to his and just idled ahead dead slow to keep the line tight.

He finally floated and there was very little damage to the hull, just a few scratches, so he ran to Port Hardy under his own power. He wanted to buy me breakfast when we got to Hardy, and gave me three hundred dollars. Over breakfast we talked.

"Where are you headed, anyway?" I asked him.

"Oh, I'm going to go right around Vancouver Island," he told me.

"Well, do you have any charts on the boat?"

"No," he says, "but I have a GPS." I had no idea what that was.

"Do you have a tide book?" I asked him.

"Oh no, I won't need a tide book."

"Well, you want to make sure you go over Nahwitti Bar at slack water or when the tide is flooding," I told him.

He replied confidently, "I do 30 knots, I don't have to worry about the tide."

"You will not be doing 30 knots over the bar if the tide is ebbing, believe me." I never did find out if he made it all the way around Vancouver Island.

Another time in Sea Otter Cove a sailboat hit the ledge going out, got stuck, and the tide was on the ebb for another two hours. I tried to pull his boat off but he was completely jammed so I waited around until the tide began to rise. As the tide rose, water began to flow into the boat and the man and woman on board were bailing like mad.

"Can't you find where the water is coming in?" I yelled, so the lady went to look and said it was coming in at the head (toilet) and the sink basin. When they got them plugged up they floated off and went on their way.

ONE EVENING AT HOME, WE HEARD A LADY IN KINGCOME INLET calling; she said she had heard a mayday call from a boat that was sinking at Cramer Island. There is no Cramer Island in the area but we all went and looked down Cramer Pass and found nothing. It was blowing a gale of southeast and I told my wife Yvonne, if the mayday had been anywhere around Cramer Pass, we would have heard it.

Bobby Lamont on *Gale Winds* was out looking and he came in to ask me what I thought.

"Well, it sure is odd that the lady in Kingcome heard the mayday, but I think it might have come from the Bond Sound area," I tell him. I got on the radio and asked if there were any tugs in the Tribune Channel area. One man answered.

"I was in Tribune around four o'clock; I passed a boat back by Kumlah Island." Bobby and I figured that must be the boat so we decided to go up Tribune. Bobby's boat was really fast so he went ahead and I got my daughters Joanie and Patty to come with me and away we went. It was rough as hell and real dark.

"What do you think, Billy," Bobby comes on the radio, "if a guy is in a life raft, where would he end up?"

"Look down on the east side of Gilford Island, there's a long rocky beach that is a real catch-all."

"Okey doke," says Bobby and heads there and lo and behold, there is a life raft on the beach and the man was safe and sound but pretty cold. His boat was an old tug type and as he was bucking the big swells off Kumlah Island the boat began to leak. It leaked so bad it began to sink. He was lucky he had a good life raft.

I heard another mayday from a prawn fisherman who said he was on Browne Rock off Isle Point at the entrance to Cramer Pass, so I ran down to Browne Rock but there was no boat. I got on the radio and asked him if he had passed Gilford Village and he said he had passed it on his port (left) side. I adjusted my search and found him on a rock at the mouth of Health Lagoon. He had hit it about an hour before low tide, and had been going slow so the boat was undamaged. I just stood by until he floated and went on his way.

Another boat that did hit Browne Rock was not so lucky. This one was a 42-foot yacht and the owner was going 16 knots when he hit it. The impact tore off one rudder and drove one propeller up through the hull. He knew he was going to sink and he managed to run it up on the beach on Gilford Island. When the tide went out I helped him tear up the floor to get at the hole and we put a patch on from the inside. We fired up a pump to get the water out, floated the boat off the beach and I towed it to Echo Bay and settled it on the beach there.

IN MY YEARS OF LISTENING TO EMERGENCY CALLS ON THE VHF radio I have heard some pretty bizarre calls. It is amazing to me how many people do not know where they are on the water, do not know how to read a chart or have a highways map instead of marine charts to navigate. One man came on with a mayday and when I inquired where he was he told me he was in Area 12—which is an area that extends from Kelsey Bay to Seymour Inlet.

Another man said, "I don't know where I am but I am on P.Y.M. rock." (Pym Rock near Echo Bay.)

And one night around 9 p.m. I got a call from a man who had run out of gas and he asked me if I could bring some gas out to his boat.

"Yup, I can do that," I told him. "Where are you?"

"Well… I am not really sure, actually."

"How the hell can I bring you gas when the big problem is you are lost?"

Most of the time I was able to help people or figure out from the wind and tide where someone might end up if they were drifting in a small or bigger boat. But one time we spent half the night looking for a boat that had been reported as overdue at its destination of Scott Cove. This boater had reported that he was at the mouth of Fife Sound at eight o'clock in the morning, heading for Scott Cove, but he never arrived. We finally gave up looking for him and he was eventually found at the mouth of Seymour Inlet, over 50 miles northwest from where we had all been looking.

THERE WERE LOTS OF PEOPLE IN SCOTT COVE FOR SEVERAL years, including families, and one night a woman was having a miscarriage. Her husband came to get me about 9 p.m. to take her to Alert Bay to the hospital. I kind of groaned inside as it was blowing about 40 knots northwest with big snow squalls. I fired up my boat and went to Scott Cove to pick her up. We laid her on a stretcher on the wheelhouse floor and her husband lay down on one side of her and a friend lay on the other side to keep her from sliding around as the boat rolled. It took us four hours to get there but she was fine in the end.

Another night around eight o'clock I got a call that a woman at a camp in Moore Bay was having a miscarriage. Of course on this dark night it was also blowing like hell and snowing, so I took off and met them in Shawl Bay, took her on board and met the Coast Guard boat *Ready* in Spring Pass. At least I did not have to roll all the way to Alert Bay that time.

Things just seemed to happen on snowy, windy nights, so I wasn't surprised when I got a call from Kingcome Village about a young Native man who had burnt his eye and was in terrible pain. He was brought down to Shawl Bay where I met up with them and I only had to go as far as Twin Lagoon this time, to meet up again with the *Ready*.

It may not have been snowy and windy every time I got a call for help but it was almost always nighttime or close to it. Around 6 p.m. I was called about a boat that was broke down off Arrow Pass. It was only blowing about 20 southeast but it was pitch black by the time I got to the boat, which had drifted out by Foster Island. The boat turned out to be a big herring punt heavily loaded with oysters from the oyster farm at Booker Lagoon.

When I take a boat in tow, the Auxiliary Coast Guard rule is that I am just supposed to tow it to the nearest safety, so my plan was to tow them to Gilford Village. These guys wanted me to tow them to Alert Bay.

"That's a hell of a long way with a big ebb tide, fellas," I told them. "A loaded punt don't tow easy. I guess I'll take you but it is going to be three hours getting there."

I saw them looking at their watches; we got to Alert Bay at 1 a.m. and they were not very happy because the bar was closed. They jumped off the boat and ran up the dock without a thank-you.

THE SCARIEST CALL I RESPONDED TO WASN'T DUE TO HIGH winds or bad weather conditions, it was the people involved.

I got a call to go check out a fish farm in Simoom Sound one evening. Coast Guard told me a worker had phoned his mother to tell her he had hurt his back really bad and said he would call her later, but he did not. She got worried and called the Coast Guard, then they called me.

So I ran out to Simoom Sound and tied up to the fish farm. There were lots of lights on and out comes a big dog trying to bite me. I waited for someone to show up but no one did, so I went up the stairs and knocked on the door. A big guy opens the door.

"Who are you and what the hell are you doing here?" he says belligerently.

"Your mom was worried about you because you didn't call her back, so she called the Coast Guard," I replied.

"Well my back is fine now."

"You gotta phone the Coast Guard and let them know you're OK," I told him.

"I'm not going to phone any — Coast Guard," he snarls.

I told him he had to but he just got madder so I got the hell out of there. I took off, called the Coast Guard and told them he was fine. If I ever get another call like that, so vague, and just to check up on some unknown person, I won't go alone. That big guy was so rude, it was obvious to me that he and the other guy there were up to no good.

AS WELL AS STRANGERS, I HAVE HELPED A LOT OF NEIGHBOURS over the years. I keep the radio on at night so I can hear if anyone calls me to go and help them. Yvonne M.'s husband Albert got a real bad infection and had to be medevacked one New Year's Day. She called the local floatplane company and had him flown out and he was in the hospital for a week. They sent him home with the wrong drugs and a few days later she called me up about four o'clock in the afternoon.

"We have to get him back to the hospital," she says. "Can you take him?"

Well, this night it was really blowing, over 70 knots southeast. Yvonne holds the boat steady at Bold Head and I go out on to the rolling deck to put the poles out. Albert is lying in the bunk groaning in pain but he gets up and comes out on deck with me to help. We had to go the long way around by Pearse Islands and just as we make the turn into Port McNeill harbour, the boat rolls over so hard the port stabilizer pole slams up into its bracket. That was a pretty hard run.

All in all, I have saved a lot of boats and a few lives, and I was happy to do it.

ALMOST EVERYONE MAKES A MISTAKE OR TWO IN THEIR LIFE-time and it's very easy for us to laugh at someone else's mistake, but when it happens to us, it's not so funny. So this is what happened to me one day in December 2014.

I had been deer hunting around the islands with no luck so I decided to run up Tribune Channel and take a walk up an old truck road where I've had good luck in past years. When I got there I tied my boat to a tree and went up the road, but there had been a big slide so I turned back and walked to the boat. Lo and behold, in the five minutes I was gone, the line had slipped off the cleat and my boat was drifting away.

I think that was the worst sinking feeling I ever had.

I stood there and swore for a bit and then I thought about what to do. I figured I had to build a raft but where I was standing I could see nothing to make a raft with. There is quite a big creek in the cove and I could see across the creek there were some slabs. So I got my tie-up line off the tree and waded across the creek. I gathered up five slabs and used the tie-up line to lash them together. By now my speedboat had been pushed about 1,200 feet offshore by the water from the creek.

I knew there was a road-building crew working about two miles down the shore so my first idea was to paddle the raft down to them. I climbed onto the raft and it turned out to be more stable than I'd thought it would be. I'd managed to find a nice little slab that would serve as a paddle and I started to paddle along the shore, keeping a sharp eye on my boat. I had paddled about 500 feet when all of a sudden the speedboat turned, so I knew it had stopped drifting away from me.

I paddled along the shore until I was as close as I was going to get to the boat and then I turned the raft and made a beeline for it. I was lucky it was flat calm with no wind, but it was still a pretty vulnerable feeling to be on a raft that was only five feet square with two inches of freeboard. I paddled for a very long half hour to reach my boat and I was one happy guy when I came alongside and climbed into it.

Words of wisdom: make sure the line is tied securely to the cleat on the boat.

Log Salvaging

MY FIRST TASTE OF LOG SALVAGING WAS WHEN I WAS TEN YEARS old; I would tow in a small fir wood log or sometimes a boomstick would float by and I would row out to tow it in. Back then there were lots of logs drifting around and you could pick up as many as you needed and do what you wanted with them.

In 1960 everything changed because Gulf Log Salvage was formed and you had to have a log salvage permit. This permit cost five hundred dollars the first year and two hundred and fifty dollars each year thereafter. You had to turn the logs in to Gulf Log and they paid you for them. You would get 60 percent for logs with no mark or stamp on them and 40 percent for marked logs. The logger who had marked the log and lost it would get the 60 percent.

Bucking a salvaged log, showing the "unique number" required by Forestry to prove I didn't fall the tree or buck off a stamp. Seven is my lucky number so I always start my numbering from 700. PHOTO BY SCOTT ROGERS

This situation caused a bit of skullduggery to ensue, as some fellows would cut off the end of a marked log to get rid of the mark. Consequently I would see a lot of little blocks with a stamp on them floating around. Because of this, you had to apply for a root bucking permit when you got logs that had roots on them, say from a landslide. You had to spray paint a number on the log and nearby on the root, and take a picture of it, then buck the root off between the numbers. This was a good idea to my mind, because it proved you had not cut off the end of a marked log, nor felled a tree you shouldn't have.

When you stamp a log you have to hit the end of the log really hard to make a clear impression. Forestry officers learned they could put coloured dye on the end of a cut-off log and the dye would travel up the log and show the stamp mark when they made a cut as far as ten feet further up the log.

Log salvaging is like any job. If you want to make a dollar at it you have to go out every morning rain or shine; you can't let a little bit of weather worry you because the day you don't go out is the day the logs go by. Or there might have been a landslide

Every log salvager has to have his own stamp hammer to stamp his number on the end of salvaged logs. My number is 928 and it has had a lot of use.

in the night and if you go out the day following the day after the slide, someone else already has the logs.

I have seen a few guys come and think they are going to make a fast buck but it doesn't work that way. Some mornings you go out and don't even get one log and it might go like that for a week. Then you go out one morning and there are logs all over the place. That's all part of the game.

On the mornings when there are logs all over, hell—you run around like mad tying them up anywhere and you spray paint your permit number on them. Once you have your number on it, it is yours. In all the years I have been log salvaging I have had only one bunch of logs stolen.

Some guys like to pick up just the big logs but I pick up any log I think is merchantable, even if it is only worth ten dollars; if you get ten logs worth ten dollars you have one hundred dollars. These days if you get what they call "low grade drift," which is low-floating logs or deadheads, you get 100 percent of the value, so they add up, too.

I love log salvaging. I jump in my boat and go ripping out there first thing in the morning almost every day through the winter and I never know what I will see or what I will find. I have picked up lots of good rope, planks, old boats, all kinds of boards, boom chains and tons of all kinds of plastic garbage, which I gather up. Old tarps, oil cans, plastic water bottles—the list goes on. Once I saw a long bright pink thing and when I got up to it, it turned out to be a big pink dildo. I just had to leave that thing behind; I couldn't picture a place for it among the stone tools or trapping or logging gear. Another day I picked up two wheelbarrows from a fish farm and a lot of big grey garbage buckets and pike poles.

Stowing the logs in the boom with a pike pole. PHOTO BY SCOTT ROGERS

Sometimes I see some interesting wildlife like a swimming bear or a wolf or cougar on the shore, and the best is a beautiful morning with a few streaky clouds in the sky turning pale pink and the sun not yet up, with a little westerly making the air smell good.

Salvage Rites

SALVAGING STUFF FROM ABANDONED LOGGING SHOWS WAS KIND of a way of life for many small loggers on the coast. As soon as a logger moved out to another claim, anything left behind was up for grabs; so this is where salvage rights come in. I call it "performing salvage rites" because salvaging items from around abandoned logging shows was like a ritual that so many of us took part in.

First, a list of tools needed to perform salvage rites: a long pike pole to fish up lost boom chains, a grapple hook to fish up boom chains that are too deep to reach with the pike pole, and a good strong magnet is a handy item. You need a spike bar to pull railroad spikes, a good wrench, a screwdriver, a hammer, a three-foot-long quarter-inch steel rod, and a gunny sack to pack things in.

I will explain as I go along what these various tools were used for.

Years ago some of these small loggers were running on a shoestring, so to speak, so when there was a chance of finding something for free, that was good news. Consequently when a camp moved location it was a small race to see who could get there first. Most camps worked six days a week so that left Sunday for the performance of salvage rites. Not every logger performed salvage rites; some felt it was a waste of time. But then there were the ones who would close their camp to be the first ones to the site. This would depend on which camp had moved, because you got to know which camp would be most likely to leave good stuff behind. Many of the smaller outfits could not afford to leave anything behind so it wasn't worth bothering to go look.

If the camp that moved was just an A-frame show you only had to look along the shore at low tide for boom chains or lost shackles. If they had boomed their logs in a shallow bay, it was a good bet you'd find boom chains or maybe even a peavey.

Skyline shows were the best place to perform salvage rites. You would go up to where the spar tree had been. Around the base of the spar tree was a good place to find shackles, shackle pins or railroad spikes. First you just walked around looking and then you walked around again, dragging the magnet. After the magnet, the steel rod was put to use. You went around a likely spot probing into the ground with the rod until you hit metal. Then you would dig.

With any luck, one of these methods would produce some goodies.

The next place to look was where the gas donkey had sat. This was a good place to find a wrench or some sort of tool or nuts and bolts, or a can of oil or grease. If you were really lucky you might even find a grease gun. Forty-five gallon drums were always a great find.

Once you had done all of the above, it was time to go and find the guy line stumps. Each spar tree had six guy lines to hold it up. These were attached to stumps about 120 feet from the base of the spar tree. The guy lines were made from one-and-an-eighth or one-and-a-quarter steel cable, so it was a sure bet you'd find some railroad spikes.

When first set up, the stump was notched with an axe and then the guy line was wrapped around the stump and held in the notch while it was pulled tight with a line from the machine. Once it was tight, six or eight railroad spikes were driven in to hold it and then a second and third wrap was put on. So these stumps always had spikes left in them. Sometimes when taking the guy line off it was easier to bend the spikes out of the way than it was to pull them out. These stumps were also a good place to find an axe, a spike bar or a sledgehammer.

Wherever there was a spar tree, there would be the skyline—a one-and-a-half or one-and-three-eighths cable that ran from the top of the spar tree to the top of the A-frame, a distance of 1,000 to 1,400 feet. The skyline ran through a thing at the top of the spar tree called a skyline jack or shoe. After the skyline was run through the jack it was then run to a stump and spiked, like the guy lines. This stump had to be good and solid and sometimes there had to be two stumps together to hold the strain that was put on the skyline while logging. So around these stumps you might find a block or a strap or a pass line chain. A pass line chain is a very strong chain with a big hook on one end and a ring on the other end, which is used to tighten the cables. Four around a stump would hold; less than four and the cable would slip.

People who perform salvage rites are in a class all their own. They can go out and spend a whole day looking for things they don't really need; they are quite happy to just be out there looking. I can speak to this as it shows in my museum. I have gone out to dig for bottles and dug and probed for hours, cut my fingers to the bone on broken glass, but if I find one good bottle I come home happy.

And take looking for railroad spikes, which I needed for my boat ways. You have to take a 50-pound spike bar and an 8-pound sledgehammer, then climb a sidehill 1,000 or 1,500 feet up, to look for some spikes that you could buy for fifty cents apiece. But you go and plow around all day and come home with a dozen spikes happy as hell.

The next good place to perform salvage rites was to look around the outer edge of the slash where they would have hung blocks for the haulback line. Sometimes the loggers kept a spare block and strap here, which would quite often be left behind. In this area you would also look for extensions of straw-line, which were three-eighths cable 200 feet long with a hook in each end. These extensions were dragged in a big loop around the area to be logged, starting at the machine and ending at the machine. They were used to pull the big cables around and sometimes one of them would get left behind.

Another good place to look was where they had moved the machine up the hill to the spar tree. This was an easy trail to follow and often things like tools, cans of oil or grease would fall off as the machine was moving, and sometimes there was a second trail to poke around in, if they had moved the machine out a different trail than the way they came in.

Years ago there were lots of small logging shows in this area, and there was also the odd big camp like Charles Creek Log in Kingcome Inlet. When this camp closed down and moved out, salvage rites were a whole new ball game. This camp was a big truck logging camp on land, with miles of road. The actual camp consisted of four bunkhouses, a cookhouse, a wash house and drying room, and a big workshop. The camp also had a sawmill, a power plant shed and two family houses. Also there were old trucks, a D8 Cat and numerous old motors in the big "boneyard" where they dumped worn-out equipment.

When the camp moved out they took the bunkhouses, the cookhouse and the wash house. Everything else was left behind. So going to Charles Creek to perform salvage rites was like going shopping to a building supply and hardware store combined. In the shop were cubbyholes full of new nuts, and bolts of all sizes. There were V belts and motor parts, cans of oil and grease and lots of 45-gallon drums, some of which were full of gas. There were doors and windows, sinks and toilets. Three big fuel tanks remained, with some diesel fuel in them. The shop itself was 60 feet wide and 100 feet long and except for one side the roof and walls were all covered with aluminum roofing.

The first time I went to Charles Creek I found so much good stuff I could not bring it all home in my speedboat so I hid some in the bush to pick up at a later date, but someone else found it. So much for being greedy. There were boom chains all along the beach at low tide and cables with shackles around trees, and railroad spikes and staples everywhere. There were even sacks of new spikes and staples in the shop.

One day I went deer hunting to Charles Creek. I took my motorbike and went about six miles up the road. On the way I performed my salvage rites by stopping at each landing where the machines had sat and where they had loaded the logging trucks. I must say I spent more time looking for things than I did looking for deer. At one landing I found a wire cutter and a sack with about fifty new railroad spikes in it. So I put them on a log to pick up on my way out. I drove to the end of the road but never saw a deer and on my way out I stopped to pick up the spikes and cutter, but they were gone.

I didn't know what to think. I had been sure I was the only one in the valley but I must have been wrong. There was no sign of anyone down at the beach. This kind of bothered me. I felt someone must have watched me put the spikes and cutter on the log and it made my hair stand up as I thought about it.

It wasn't until four years later when I was up Kingcome talking to a man who worked in the camp there. I told him about my incident at Charles Creek and he started to laugh. What happened was he had come up the road about an hour behind me on his bike and seen the spikes and cutter sitting on the log. As he saw no deer sign he had taken the spikes and cutter and gone home, so he was long gone by the time I came back down to the beach.

About a year after Charles Creek was abandoned I decided to build a new boat shed at Echo Bay and I thought all the aluminum on the shop at Charles Creek would make my roof. I got a friend to go with me to salvage the aluminum. When we got there, we could not believe what we saw.

The shop had 12 x 12 posts about 12 feet apart and someone had cut 3-inch strips of rubber from a truck tire inner tube and made a giant slingshot and used all the nuts and bolts for ammunition and shot the aluminum full of holes. They didn't miss a single sheet. Whoever did this must have worked like hell because my guess is there were over five hundred holes in the aluminum and the slingshot needed a real pull to stretch it out.

One day my wife and I went on a salvage expedition. We were living on a floathouse out in Knight Inlet and we were after a good piece of cable for a shore line. I had been told about a guy line that had been left up the hillside at Harry Bay in the mouth of Kingcome Inlet. I was also told that this guy line had been burnt. This is not like being burnt in a fire; it had been stretched around a small object and was like a coiled spring.

So up the hill we go and find the guy line about 300 feet up the hill with both ends running down the hill. The bight was around some trees so we had to pull one end up the hill to clear it of the trees. Try pulling a one-and-a-quarter-inch cable that is full of kinks up a hill. Once we got it all straight we worked one end down to the shore so I could get a rope from my boat and use the boat to pull the cable down the hill.

Well, the idea was good but I had forgotten the water was 300 feet deep so I had 300 feet of heavy cable hanging off the stern of my boat. So, what to do? I had to find some shallow water so I made for the head of Cypress Harbour until I was in about eight feet of water and then we pulled the cable aboard little by little.

That was one piece of wire I really worked for. Yvonne, too.

When I bought the boat shed in Echo Bay there was no railroad track. The ties were there but the track had been taken so I needed some rails. I knew there were a lot at Cockatrice Bay so I got two friends to go and help me get the rails. When we got to Cockatrice we found that all the rails close to the beach were gone so we had to go back up in the bush 400 feet. First we pulled out a box of railroad spikes, then we had to take the rails apart—which was no easy task. We worked all day and only had two rails free because all the nuts were rusted and we had to chisel them off.

Next we tried to drag the rails down to the beach but it was almost impossible to move as they weighed 400 pounds apiece, so we came home sort of defeated. I had to come up with a plan. From time to time I went out and worked at getting the rails freed up. After four trips I had twelve rails ready to go. Getting them to the beach was the next problem. I knew once I got them there, if I left them long enough, someone else would take them. It was

February and the weather turned for a cold spell and some of the camps closed down.

Three of my friends said, "Let's go get your rails, Bill." Away we went and I picked up a big cedar log on the way, to float the rails home with.

This was one salvage rite that I was really prepared for. I had ropes and blocks and even had a rail carrier. We tried to use the rail carrier to move the rails down to the beach but it was no good because the ties were frozen solid and once we got a rail to start moving it would not quit and would run us down. To deal with this problem we tied a rope to the rail alone, and ran like hell to keep ahead of it. We had all the rails down to the beach in less than two hours. This was one time that the weather really made a difference in helping me perform salvage rites.

When we had all the rails at the beach, we rolled them into a bundle and tied strong ropes around them and waited until the tide covered them. Then I floated the cedar log over the rail bundle, tied the ropes around the log, attached the works to the boat's tow rope, pulled the load off the beach and headed home.

Boat Ways Blues

IN 1958 I BOUGHT A BOAT REPAIR SHOP IN ECHO BAY. IT CON-sisted of a shed, an old Petters lighting plant that put out 7,000 watts DC, a band saw, a jointer and the railroad ties where the haulout for boats had been. The man I bought it from, my wife's cousin Ralph Roth, had sold the railroad track, and the winch, motor and cradle, which are the essential elements of a boat ways, to someone else. All I got was the bare bones.

So the first thing I had to do was get some railroad track, a winch and a motor. There was all that track out at Cockatrice Bay, which my friends helped me get.

I needed twelve rails as well as a large number of railroad spikes, plus twelve fish plates (which join the railroad tracks together) and bolts. The spikes were no problem but the fish plates were a pain. Each fish plate has four bolts and they were rusted up pretty good, so it was a chisel job with a lot of swearing and skinned knuckles before I had my twelve plates.

The ties on the shore below the ways were still good and solid so after we towed the tracks home I got them spiked in place pretty easily. Next I needed wheels and a cradle. The cradle was no problem. I went to Telegraph Cove to get the timbers I needed. It was a special order though so I had to wait two months until they could be cut. I needed four 8 x 12 timbers 36 feet long and six 8 x 8 timbers 16 feet long. The timbers were finally cut and I towed them home so all that was left to get were the wheels. Some of the old-timers told me where I could find some and I took a look but they were all too big. I decided I'd better buy some.

A place called Nye's Foundry in Vancouver made wheels just for boat ways. They weighed 87 pounds each. I ordered eight. They only cost fifteen dollars each but the freight cost was twenty dollars each. When I got them, they had only a rough-cast hole in the centre so I had to take them to Alert Bay Shipyards and get the holes turned out in their lathe and two-inch shafts put in. This cost eighty-five dollars per wheel. So for a total of nine hundred and sixty (plus a lot of running around) I had my wheels. The shafts were free.

It was 1958 when I was trying to put together this ways. I was twenty-four years old, only just married and almost flat broke, so I had to really spend my money carefully.

Next on the list were bolts, and lots of them, plus sixteen bearings for the wheels, which I made out of yew wood. Sixteen bearings required thirty-two bolts, 18 inches long by five-eighths or three-quarters and I needed twenty bolts, 22 inches long by five-eighths or three-quarters, plus sixteen bolts, 20 inches long by five-eighths or three-quarters. So where to find sixty-eight bolts? Well, the large spools that big cable comes on have six to eight bolts in them that are five-eighths of an inch, so I went to all the old log dumps and I found all the bolts I needed, but they were all too long. I had to cut them to the right length and put a thread on them.

After that, I had everything I needed to build the cradle for my boat ways.

Two weeks later I had the cradle built and then I needed a winch. There were some big winches around but they were all *too* big so I went to see Fred Pedersen and by God, he had just what I needed. It was an old steam winch off a boat that used to trawl for shrimp. There was one problem though: it was made of cast iron, which meant it was strong but could not withstand any sudden jerks or it would break. I decided I could live with that.

I got the winch in place and bolted down and the next thing was a motor. I got a six-cylinder Chev for free from a man in Alert Bay and after I got that installed I turned my attention to the shed.

The shed was just part of the old shingle mill building, a big framework affair built out of 12 x 12 fir timbers all bolted together, but they were rotten so I had to build a whole new shed. First I had to tear down the old one, which was a big job as there was about

20,000 board feet of timbers in it. I got a big fire going and cut from the top down. It took ten days to get it all burnt and the site prepared to build the new shed on. Off I went to Telegraph Cove to buy 6,000 board feet of lumber, which required three trips to haul it all. The shed was to be 28 feet by 56 feet so I needed two nice long cedars for the foundation. I hand logged a couple and pulled them into place with the winch. I planned to build a Quonset type of building so I made arches out of 1 x 4, stood them up and sheathed them over with shiplap.

Next I needed something for the roof. I knew the big shop that was left at Charles Creek had many sheets of aluminum roofing. There was more roofing than I needed but, as mentioned, someone had punched most of it full of holes with a giant slingshot. It took us two days to get enough for my roof, and most of it had holes in it but I took the pieces home and patched the holes with tar.

When I bought the shop it was on five acres of land that was a lease with a special use permit or SUP, which was for boat repair only. Shortly after I bought the ways, the Forest Service, which had their houses and office in what is now Echo Bay Park, wanted the back part of the five acres to make a baseball field. Then the school wanted a six-foot-wide strip designated for a trail to the school. The lease was only forty-five dollars per year, payable to Forestry, so the community decided they wanted to build a hall on my five acres. I gave them the bit where the hall still stands and I ended up with a lot 40 x 90 feet in size.

When the shingle mill was in operation they had a big sawdust burner built out of bricks. When the mill moved out they left the big pile of bricks in place and sold the power plant to Telegraph Cove. Ralph Roth and Rod Wallace had built the boat shop in 1946 and bought the power plant back from Telegraph Cove. One year they neglected to pay the lease to Forestry so the pile of bricks was seized. When I took over the lease, it was written on the lease agreement that I was NOT to remove or alter the pile of bricks as they were property of the Crown. When we built the community hall we had to get a permit to flatten out the pile of bricks, so the hall is built over that pile of bricks.

Once I got the building up and roofed, and all the track, cradle, winch and motor in place, I was open for business. The whole process took almost four years.

March 16, 1962, I pulled the first boat up on the ways and that was the start of a twenty-two-year operation on the shore of Echo Bay. For the first year or so the boat ways worked well but then one day I went to pull up a boat called *Alice* and there was not enough water. I pulled the cradle back and put the boat on. Unbeknownst to me, the cradle had come off the track. I got the boat partway up and could not pull it any further. I tried to let it back down but had no luck with that either. It was *stuck*, as the wheels hung up on the ties and completely jammed.

So I had to wait until the tide fell to see what to do. This was the first time the cradle had come off the track; little did I know then it would be a common occurrence, at least once a year. When the tide went out, I got some jacks and jacked the cradle and boat back onto the track; luckily *Alice* was a small boat. So after that little episode I was very careful whenever I pulled the cradle up.

Alice was owned by Yalmer Mittinnen, a real nice Finlander who stuttered; he was known as the Stuttering Finn. He was a troller, a good fisherman, and he took good care of his boat. It had a two-cylinder Easthope for power. The first time I met Yalmer I asked him what kind of motor he had.

"Ma donk, ma donk," he said; he was making the sound an Easthope makes because he was not able to say the word. He called his rowboat an "oar-o-let." Yalmer played the accordion and was damn good at it but he only played when he was half drunk. So when his boat was stuck on my ways, he got in his oar-o-let, rowed over to the Echo Bay Pub and had a few beers. He rowed back and sat on the deck of *Alice* all the time I was jacking the cradle back on the track. I should mention here that Yalmer was sixty-eight years old, a bit overweight and not too good on his feet.

The next thing that happened (it seems I was not careful enough) was I had to put *Sun Dog* on the ways. It was a 48-foot tug that belonged to Frank Beban, a deep heavy boat, and I knew it was too big for my ways. We tried to get it on the cradle but there was not enough water.

So Frank says, "I will pull the cradle back a bit."

"For God's sakes, take it easy," I tell him. He backed it down a bit and everything seemed all right but when I went to pull the cradle up, it was off the track. Well, this was serious because I knew there was no way I could jack the cradle back on the track with this heavy boat on it.

Frank says, "I'll just back off," and he backed up full bore but the boat did not move. He had a towing winch so I took the towing line and ran it across the bay with my speedboat, and tied it to a tree. The plan was, I would pull on the winch line and back up at the same time and the boat would come off.

The whole time we are doing this the tide is falling. Frank put the winch in gear and the motor full speed astern and *Sun Dog* never moved. What to do? The tide was going to be two feet higher at 1 a.m. so I said we should leave it until then and I could get it off for sure.

"Run in the winch line, Frank," I said and went and cut it loose. He was running it in and it hooked on something, so he speeded the motor up to give the winch more power. What was happening was the eye in the end of the winch line had hooked over the end of one of the tracks, and when he went ahead the track was pulled up out of the water. Frank was watching the winch, not the line, so before my yelling stopped him, there were three lengths of track and all the ties hanging in the air. When Frank saw that, he ran out of the ways, jumped in his speedboat and took off for Charles Creek.

When the tide was full out, it was a sight to behold. The rails and ties were hanging in the air but the worst part was there was a six-foot by twenty-foot trench about six feet deep in the beach, dug by the prop wash. The tide came in high at one in the morning and the boat floated off the cradle and I towed it to the forestry dock in Echo Bay. The biggest job was to fill the hole so I could put the ties back in place. It took me two days of shovelling to fill the hole and another two days to lay the ties back. Two of the tracks were bent too badly to re-use and four fish plates were ruined. Luckily I had two spare tracks, but no fish plates, so I ran out to Cockatrice Bay for more fish plates. All in all it took me six days to get the ways back in shape, partly because I could only work at low tide.

I got *Sun Dog* back on the cradle and all went well this time so I scrubbed it off and copper painted it. I charged ten dollars to haul out and if I did the work it was two dollars an hour for labour. So ten dollars for the haulout, plus two dollars an hour for fourteen hours labour, plus fourteen dollars for the paint comes to fifty-two dollars. For that work I don't think I was ever paid.

A lot of folks did not like to pay ten dollars to get hauled out. One man who lived in Echo Bay and always knew when the ways was empty would wait until there was a boat on it and would come over and say, "Well I would sure like to get on the ways tomorrow but I see it is being used, so I guess I will have to put my boat on the beach."

Which he did, every year. He set his boat right by the ways and let it lean uphill and would paint one side, then turn it around and paint the other side, complaining all the while about how he could not get on the ways.

There were two guys who went on the ways every year in May, but they would not pay when they went on. They would come see me about going on the ways and then they would pay me for last year. And there were others who never paid at all. They would wait until I was away fishing and they would pull their boats up themselves.

One time I came home and my wife Yvonne said, "Something is wrong with the boat ways." So I went to have a look and everything looked alright except the cradle was down. I went to pull it up and then I found the winch was broken in about four pieces, completely ruined. I knew Fred Pedersen had another one the same as the one I had, so off I went to see Fred and told him about the winch.

"I told you to be real careful with it or you would bust it," says Fred.

"I didn't do it, I was away fishing and someone else did it," I told him.

"You can have the winch but do not let anyone else use it, Bill."

I got the new winch set up and everything was back in place, or so I thought, but when I went to pull the cradle up it resisted coming up and was bouncing up and down. I got it up and took a look and there were two broken wheels.

To me, the really sad part about this is that no one said a word about it to me. Eventually I did find out what took place. A couple of guys pulled one boat up and then went to let the cradle down, at low tide. This is something one should *never* do for any reason; there needs to be enough water to float the boat and release it from the cradle on which it is resting. So the boat and cradle went flying down the track and they slammed on the brake to try to stop it and the sudden shock broke the winch. The cradle would have run right off the track but I had placed some rocks at the end of the track to stop this from happening. It was going so fast with the boat on it that the wheels broke when they hit the rocks.

After that I put on a boom chain and padlocked it so no one could use it while I was away fishing. I did not like to do this because the ways could be handy in an emergency, if someone's boat was leaking badly or sinking, so I left the key with someone I could trust. Things went smoothly for almost a year, but then one day I came home from fishing and Yvonne told me, "There's a fire at the boat ways." I ran over there and found a guy with a big bonfire right by the cradle, and between the tracks.

"What the hell do you think you are doing?" I yelled.

"What the f—— is that to you?" he replies.

"I own this outfit and I don't want it to burn down!" I said. "Get this fire out right now and get the hell off my property!"

I was standing by the winch and he jumped on the cradle and yelled, "*You* or no one else is going to make me!"

So I picked up a piece of 2 x 4 and said, "You s.o.b. get out of my shed right now or you will be sorry!" He called me a few sweet names and he did put the fire out, but then he lit another one just down the beach a bit.

A lot of people have said to me over the years how lucky I am to have my own boat ways. I don't know about the luck part because it has been one heck of a lot of work to keep it in shape, but it is handy.

One day I went to start the power plant. It was old and often hard to start. Like the old Hot Head my Dad had, you had to light a blowtorch to heat up the head, then crank like hell. This day it started right away but only ran a short time, then stopped. I gave it a crank and discovered it was seized. It had an oiler on its side to oil all the moving parts. The oiler held about a gallon of oil but I noticed there was a clam shell on top of the oiler. I looked under the clam shell and the oiler was full of sand.

The Forest Service homes were right next door and the kids used to play in the boat shed when it was raining. I went and asked the mothers if any of their little dears had come home all oily. One four-year-old named Bobby Brash, the head ranger's son, was the culprit. That boy was a little demon who could do no wrong.

So much for my power plant; nothing that a thousand dollars wouldn't replace. Shortly after the power plant episode I was under the cradle copper painting and dear little Bobby came along and picked up some sawdust and threw it at me. I just ignored him so he picked up some sand and threw that. I told him to go home, and then he picked up an egg-sized rock and threw that. It hit me on the head and I was out from under that boat like a shot and caught him as he was running out the door. I gave him an earful, towed him to his house and gave his dad hell. I thought he might be mad at me but he never said a word.

When there was a party going on in the hall, a lot of drinking went on in my shed, mostly by the teenagers. After every party I would find bottles hidden among the lumber. The kids would also smoke in the shed. I was always afraid of fire but they never caused one.

When the cradle was newly built I had two chocks that were on a slide, which could be pulled in to the sides of the hull to hold a boat from tipping over. When a fellow got his boat on the cradle I would pull it up until the keel sat on the cradle and then pull the chocks in. One day I had an old boat to pull up; it was a bit rotten so I knew I had to be careful. I began to pull it up and noticed the bow coming high out of the water so I stopped. The guy who was on the boat told me the boat had sat down so he pulled the chocks in. Turns out the boat had not settled down onto the cradle before he pulled the chocks in and that put the weight of the boat on the chock. As the boat was pulled up the track, the chock punctured the hull, breaking three planks and four ribs. It took me five days to fix that one. The boat was so rotten there was no place to start from, so that was another lot of work for no pay.

Things went smooth for another period with no major problems, except for that when the winch and wheels had been broken I had replaced the wheels with two that were too light for the job. One other had a crack so I ordered four new ones. I had to lift the cradle up about two feet to get underneath and get the old bolts out, remove the broken wheels, and bolt the new ones in. So the cradle was like new again and I had a spare wheel.

About once a year I would pull up the Forestry boats and most of them were not too heavy, until they got a new boat that was 50 feet long. They wanted me to pull it up and I told them it was too heavy for my cradle. They were sure it would be OK though and convinced me to try. I waited for a real high tide, they put the boat on the cradle and I pulled it up a little and left it while the tide fell.

No one told me that it had been a sailboat, which had a curved keel, so instead of sitting on five cross skids, it sat on only three. The bow was two feet up from the front skid so I set a jack between the front skid and the keel to take some of the weight, propped it up well and went home. Just when I got home I heard a huge crash from over by the ways so I ran like hell back over there, all the time thinking the cradle had broken or the boat had rolled over. When I

Forestry boat Nesika on the cradle at my ways in Echo Bay. This is the boat seen in the 1963 National Film Board of Canada movie "The Water Dwellers", a story about the Echo Bay Forest Service and their role in the coastal community, particularly in fighting forest fires. PHOTO BY BILL PROCTOR

got there everything was fine. A young ranger had made the noise just to scare me. Well, he sure did.

After a while I got an old bunkhouse and moved it up alongside my shed to store lumber in and I bought another old Petter power plant and wired the shed so I would have some lights. I planned to be gone fishing for ten days and a fellow told me he'd like to do some work on his boat, some sanding and painting. He asked me to pull his boat up before I went so I did and I showed him how to run the power plant.

When I came home I went to see how things were at the boat shed, because it had got so I never knew what to expect, except that there was bound to be something. The boat was gone and the cradle was down at the end of the track so I went to pull the cradle back up but the battery was dead. I had a battery charger so I went to start the power plant but it would not start. It had to be hand cranked as it had no starter and it was stiff as hell to roll over. I checked the oil and there was none. I had told the man that the plant was old and burned some oil so to be sure to check the oil level every day. I had left two gallons of oil by the plant, which was still sitting there. I filled the power plant up with oil and got it going but it smoked like crazy and was making a knocking noise so I shut it off and left it for a later date. Went home and got another battery and pulled the cradle up.

The next day I went to visit the guy who had had his boat on the ways when I went fishing and he said he had used the plant for eight days and it had run well. I had to do a little question asking around the neighbourhood but I finally found out what had taken place. There had been three people working on the boat and all smoking a bit of pot. The plant started to smoke a bit too and make loud knocking noises, then it quit. I guess they had tried to restart it but it was seized from lack of oil so, even though they were not done, they let the boat down. Then they tried to pull the cradle back up and killed the battery trying to get the motor going, which they might have done if they had put some gas in the tank. All this for a ten-dollar haulout and five dollars a day for the use of the power plant and tools. And once again, I was never paid.

About this time my wife and her sister decided they'd like to put in a small garden because we were all living on floats at that time. I dug up an area about 12 x 20 feet and built a fence around it to keep out the deer. They planted their seeds and things were growing just fine when I got a letter from the Department of Lands saying, "We have been informed that you have a garden by your boat shed and we will have you know the Special Use Permit is for a boat repair shop only and can NOT be used for agriculture." So much for the garden. We tore down the fence and six months later I got another letter saying, "We have been informed you have a bunkhouse on the land and we will tell you again, the land is for a boat repair shop and nothing else. Any more violations and you will be fined up to one thousand dollars." I could see I needed to keep a low profile or else. I knew who the informer was. They were tied in Echo Bay, and she loved writing complaining letters. As my mother said, "She should learn to keep her own nose clean."

I ignored the letter about the bunkhouse because if they ever sent anyone to look at it, they would have seen how ridiculous the whole thing was. Things were good for about a year and a half and then I went away fishing, but I forgot to lock up the cradle. The same ones who broke the winch once before decided to go ahead and pull their boats up; there were three of them. I guess they got one boat up and down with no problem but boat number two tipped the cradle and it came off the track. They didn't know it was off until they went to pull it up. They got it partway up and then the winch would not pull anymore.

So they revved up the motor and jumped on the friction brake and guess what—another broken winch.

This time they only cracked the frame and were able to bolt it together but they still had to get the cradle back on the track with a very heavy boat sitting on it. They managed it but did a lot of damage to it with the jack, tearing big chunks off the timbers. They told me the use of the ways should be free because I was not there and they did all the work.

After that I made absolutely sure no one could use the ways. Some folks were real upset about this but too bad. I'd had enough of people destroying my ways and walking away without paying.

I replaced all the bearings after about ten years plus one more cracked wheel, which was a six-day job. The next bad episode was with a man named Bruce Smith, a hippy who lived in the old store building in Echo Bay. Bruce had a 20-foot lifeboat and wanted to make a sailboat out of it. This meant he would have to put a deep keel on it so I pulled the boat up in January, knowing he would be there a long time. I lifted the boat up into the shed and let the cradle down so I could use it if I had to. I would go over every few days to see how he was doing but he spent more time smoking pot and meditating than he did working. About a month went by and I had to pull a boat up that was leaking badly.

I pulled that boat up and the owner wanted me to fix it. I was working booming logs at the time so I would go over after I finished that work to work on the boat. Three days after I pulled the boat up Bruce comes over to see me and he wants off the ways right now. I told him I needed at least one more day to fix the other boat. He tells me he can't wait that long. I guess I got a bit mad.

He said, "I am going over and letting the other boat down." And he took off so I dropped what I was doing and ran like hell over to the ways. I got there before he did and I waited to see what he was going to do. He was pretty shocked when he saw me there. I told him I would have the other boat ready at high tide the next day; that I'd let it down and then pull the cradle up for him, but he would have to raise his boat two feet so the cradle would fit under it. He got an old guy to give him a hand lifting his lifeboat. They were using two jacks and I could see what was going to happen. I told them but they did not heed what I said.

So the boat rolled over, as I had warned them, and one of the jacks went right through the bottom. We finally got the cradle under it, but of course it had a big hole in it.

Bruce says, "I guess you are going to let my boat down and it will sink now."

"Nope," I said, "I will give you twenty-four hours to get it fixed and get all your junk out of my shed and I don't ever want to see you again." I gave him a bill for twenty-eight dollars and he gave me twenty-eight one dollar bills.

"You are taking my life savings," he said.

The cracked winch finally fell apart and had to be replaced and I found an old boom winch that was a bit haywire, but it was all steel and strong. So I put it in place and it worked well. In the twenty-two years I only had one boat roll over and that was *Senator 2*, owned by George Smith, the teacher's husband. It was an old 36-foot cabin cruiser. I pulled it up into the shed. I always took a walk down alongside to make sure a boat was sitting OK,

BILLY'S LIFE STORIES ◆

but this day, I went to turn on the water for the hose and while I was doing that, the boat rolled over. If I had done what I had done so many times before it would have rolled right on top of me. That was one day my guardian angel was watching over me. When the boat rolled, a 4 x 4 timber went through the side and broke three planks and two ribs.

The first big job was to get the boat back on an even keel, which is hard to do with an old wooden boat. You have to be real careful you don't put the jack through the bottom. We got the boat upright and braced and then I had to put in new ribs and three new planks, which took two days. So, one day to get it upright, two days to repair the damage, all for no pay. Times like this I would ask myself, *why am I doing this?* I should close down the ways or just have it for my own use. But I kept operating the thing for years.

After eighteen years of operation, the land around my lease was turned into Echo Bay Provincial Marine Park. So I got a letter from the Parks Department informing me I would have to pay $2,500 per year. This was one heck of a jump from $45 per year and much more than the ways made in a year. I wrote them a letter saying I could not pay that much and I also asked Forestry to write because they were still using the ways each year for their boats. They wrote me back stating I must pay or move off the land. We wrote back and forth for about two years until I got a final letter stating that I had two weeks to get off the land or they would send someone in to remove everything and restore the land to its original shape. And that I would have to pay all costs or I could be fined up to $10,000.

That was the last straw. They had me over a barrel, it was move or else.

I wrote again and said I would get off just as soon as I could but it was going to be a big job removing the track and shed and bunkhouse. The reply said the two weeks will be extended to one month from the date of this letter, at which time you will send us some pictures showing that the land has been restored to its original shape.

First I took a big log over and let the cradle down and tied the log to it to float it. I had moved onto land by then, where I am now, and I towed the cradle over and put it on the beach. Then I tore up the track and ties, moved the bunkhouse onto a float, and then the shed. The whole time I was doing this, I was also working so I was burning a lot of midnight oil. I got the shed on a bunch of loose logs and towed it over to my bay and tied it to the boom.

There was a big hole in the bank at Echo Bay beach, where the cradle had sat, so I took my tractor over and spent two days gathering anything I could find to fill the hole and then covered it all with dirt. That's the way it is today, only now it is covered with white clam shell again.

It's too bad really, just another end to the era in Echo Bay, and a senseless one at that; rules made by someone who had never set foot in the community or on the beach there.

I took all the letters I had received from the Parks Department and put them in a big envelope with a note stating, "In twenty-two years I have hauled up over seven hundred boats and a lot of them were government boats, so I hope you are happy now. As for the pictures, I am not sending any because I am sure you will be informed because it seems you have been informed about everything else I have done in the last twenty-two years." I never heard another word from them.

So I had the cradle and rails over where I live, but there was no good place to build a railway; too many big boulders. I went to work with my tractor and at low tide I pushed the boulders aside and cleared a strip where I could lay the track. I needed about forty ties so I chose a low floating hemlock and some alder to make them out of. Two weeks later the track was laid and the cradle was on it but I had no winch as I had left the old one at Echo Bay.

I made up my mind that this time I was not going to pull up other people's boats; the ways would be for my use only. That plan was soon forgotten and I was back to pulling up other people's boats. I used the winch on my tractor for pulling up the boats and that worked well because it had lots of power. I used that for about two years but I could see I needed a winch so I bought one with a motor for $2,500. I also needed new track.

A friend at Beaver Cove said he could get me some rails and he did, and he put them on the beach at Alder Bay. I towed a big clear log over there with *Twilight Rock*, lashed the rails to it and towed them home. Changing the rails was going be a hard job; they were 650 pounds each and were going to be hard to handle, but I did already have lots of good fish plates and bolts. I got the new rails down and bolted and the new winch in place so I was back to pulling up the odd boat. Just before I went fishing again I pulled up a sailboat for a neighbour and I told him I would be gone for a month.

"That's fine," he says. "I've got a lot of work to do." I did tell him if he decided to let the boat off to *make sure* it was high tide and I showed him how to use the brake to let it down easy. When I came home a month later I found the cradle down at the end of the track, so I went to pull it up. The winch was OK, nothing broken, and the motor was OK too. So I thought, *I am lucky this time.* But when I got the cradle up, I could see I was wrong.

On the front of the cradle there are two chains that form a bridle, so the cradle is pulled from both sides. One chain was broken and the cradle was two feet out of square, more diamond-shaped than rectangular. What happened was he let the boat down at low tide and just let it go and did not use the brake until he saw the cradle was going to run off the end of the track. So he slammed on the brake and one side of the chain broke. The cradle stopped but his boat kept on going and slid six feet off the cradle. He was lucky the boat stopped there and did not roll over.

Of course I had one hell of a time trying to pull the cradle square but I did get it close, and I put on a new chain. The cross timbers on the cradle were thirty years old by this time so I figured I should replace them. I had my own sawmill by then so I cut my own timbers, but it was back to undoing rusted bolts; lots of hack sawing, cussing, chiselling and skinned knuckles. I had lots of bolts this time so four days later the cradle was like new.

I still needed a shed to house everything and keep the rain off while I was working in there. My plan was for a shed 56 x 84 feet and high enough for the mast of a boat to fit under. I cut the lumber to make arches and my daughter Patty helped me with the foundation and floor. I constructed the arches and raised them into place with only one little setback: half the arches fell over and I had to stand them up again. The whole neighbourhood came to help put on the strapping and nail up the shakes.

Now I have everything, a good winch and good shed, good track and the cradle is good as new except for the wheels. I have to get some new wheels but they are hard to find. I priced out new ones in 1986. At the same place I had paid fifteen dollars for each wheel back in 1960, they now wanted six hundred dollars for each, which was out of my ballpark. A fellow gave me four good wheels but they had a four-inch hole, which was two inches too big for my needs. I tried to make do with them but they were always giving me trouble. One or the other was always off the track because there was just too much slack in the shaft and a few times the shaft fell right out.

I really had to get eight good wheels I could afford, so I went to Alert Bay Shipyards. They had seven new wheels for a hundred dollars each, which were just the right size with the shafts in them and were ready to put on. I made do with one wheel I had that was not too bad so I was all set, but I had gone to Alert Bay in my speedboat and it was too rough to bring back such a heavy load. The owner, Steve Gulstrum, said he would bring the wheels out to me on the first good weather day, which he did. It cost me one hundred more dollars—which, to me, was a bargain.

Once again I went through the whole process of putting wheels on the cradle. I tore off some of the decking on the cradle, removed a couple of tons of rock, jacked it up two feet and blocked it. Ground the heads off the rusted bolts and chiselled them out. After four days of this I had all the bolts off, the bearings and wheels apart, only one blood blister and two skinned knuckles, all with one heck of a lot of swearing.

I quite often questioned my own sanity, wondering why I was doing this with all the problems I've had with the ways. Forty-four years I've had it and if I had kept track of the time and the money I have probably worked for less than one cent an hour.

Now I was ready to put on the new wheels and this time the bolts only had to be cut to the right length and threaded. I did two wheels a day and when I got them on I replaced the two tons of rock in the cradle, nailed the decking back on, lowered the cradle onto the track and let it down.

It went down like a dream and back up.

So now I just sit and wait for the next disaster; I am sure it is bound to happen.

I forgot to mention one little episode. One day I was pulling up Bill McLeod's boat *Angelic Isles*. Bill was on the beach and his wife Frances was on board and the boat was just about up when the cable broke and the cradle and boat went flying down the track. When the boat hit the ocean, a wall of water rolled up the stern and into the cockpit.

Bill had tied the boat tight to the posts on the cradle and as the boat kept going the lines got tighter. The boat began to list badly and floated the cradle off the track. Frances was not a happy camper, to say the least. To start with she had not wanted to stay on the f—— boat but Bill had said she would be fine. There was poor old Frances on a boat with a 30-degree list and a lot of water in the galley that had run in from the cockpit. Old Bill was standing on the beach killing himself laughing and I was not helping matters any either. *Angelic Isles* had a door on the side of the wheelhouse and it happened to be on the side that was lower. Frances could not stand up with such a list and she crawled over to the door. When she opened it and saw how close the water was she just went wild, screaming all sorts of obscenities. Some were too awful to print and some added to my vocabulary.

Bill helped her off the boat and rented a room for her in the Echo Bay Hotel. It took him the rest of the day to cool her down. Meanwhile I got the boat untied and over to the dock. I waited until the tide dropped and lashed a cedar log to the cradle, and the next day I floated it right back onto the track.

After that little episode, whenever Bill had to go on the ways, Frances would get a room in the hotel.

One hot day I was pulling up Bobby Halliday's boat. The procedure went like this: I would pull the boat up a bit and he would scrub it off and I would pull a bit more until he was done. He was standing on the cradle and I just could not resist—I let the brake go and Bobby started to run but the cradle was too fast. He yelled, "Proctor, you son of a ——!"

I stopped the cradle just before the boat floated. I was not too popular that day.

Another time I had Cliff Ginger's boat, *Gore Rock*, up to replace the old motor with a new one. I was helping him get the old one out and something slipped and the motor hit Cliff on his heel. He took off running around the shipyard, yelling.

"She's gone, she's gone," he is howling.

"For God's sakes, take your shoe off and have a look," I say.

"It's no use, she's gone, she tore the heel right off."

When he finally slowed down I got him to sit down and take off his shoe and sock. There was no blood but just the makings of a big blood blister. Cliff looked at it and said, "Oh no, she will fall off and I will be a cripple for life." I told him it would be fine in a few days but he was having no part of it. Cliff was kind of a funny guy and I knew he was just putting on a show.

And one day I pulled Shorty Martens's boat up, with him on it. Shorty was seventy-five years old and he wanted me to paint the bottom for him. The next day I was down beside the boat painting and Shorty had to have a pee. He had a wound from World War II that had taken a bit off the head of his penis so when he peed it sprayed out sideways. It was a bit like being under a shower and when I yelled, Shorty just stood there and laughed like hell.

So those are some of my memories about the boat ways. And just recently, I received a check for three hundred dollars from a fellow named Jerry Broswick, who went on the ways over two years ago and could not pay me then. It kind of made up a bit for some of the damage people did over the years.

Deer Hunting 2012

I HAVE BEEN A DEER HUNTER FOR OVER SIXTY-FIVE YEARS. IN that time I have shot many big bucks and have packed and dragged a buck, sometimes for more than a mile, out to my boat. I have dragged them off mountains and out of the salal brush, in and out of gullies, and down logging roads. Many times when I was a long way from the beach I would wonder: *why the hell did I shoot?* Once you pull the trigger the fun is over and the work begins. When I was young it was no big deal but now I am older it is a big chore.

In November 2012 deer were hard to find on Gilford Island. I had been out almost every day for three weeks and had seen only one deer. It was getting late in the season and I was just about ready to give up and go buy 25 pounds of hamburger and call it good. I had already burnt up over four hundred dollars' worth of gas. Anyway I decided to try one more time so I went to a truck road on a nearby island that was nice and open and good walking. As I am walking along I see some real big tracks that were real fresh. I also noticed some fresh wolf and cougar tracks in places as I walked and ravens keeping a close eye on me.

Shortly, I saw a doe running, and a big buck running behind her. They both ran into the trees and I lost sight of them. I stood there and thought, *Boy I sure missed my chance to get a big buck.* But then I spotted them running along just in the trees a bit ahead of me, and the row of trees they were in came right to the edge of the road. When I got up to where the trees met the road, the doe came out and saw me so she turned around and went back into the trees.

My big mistake was that I should have waited 50 yards down the road and they both might have come back out on the road, but that's old age for you; you don't think as fast. I kept going on up the road for an hour or more, and then I saw another doe but she had no buck with her. I tried to look horns on her but no luck. I decided she must be an old maid.

So I gave up and turned back and was heading back to where I had seen the big buck and as I came around the bend in the road I spotted a doe up in the slash, about 75 yards away. I took a look at her through my scope and then I saw the big buck standing behind a stump.

I shot the buck, and dressed him out and dragged him off the slash and onto the road. It was then I realized how big he really was; by far the biggest buck I had ever shot.

At this point I am over two kilometres from the beach and a lot of the road is uphill. The first part is downhill though so I make a start dragging the buck and I can go about 100 feet before I have to stop and rest. When I get to the flat part I can only go about 60 feet before I have to rest. I was never going to be able to drag the buck uphill so I had to think about what I was going to do. Should I leave it and go get help?

It would take me half an hour to walk to the beach, another twenty minutes to go get help, twenty minutes to get back and another half hour back to the buck. So I thought about my options.

If I went for help there was a good chance a wolf or cougar would come and eat it while I was gone. All the time I was thinking things through I was dragging the buck and it was pouring down rain. If I left the deer I would have to cover it with my coat but then I would freeze. The only choice left was to cut the deer in half and drag half at a time. I had never done this before but I could not see any other way I was going to get out, with the deer, before dark.

So I cut it in half through the ribs. That part was easy but the backbone was a bit tougher. I finally got my knife into the backbone and drove it through by pounding the knife with a rock. Now that I had two pieces to drag the going was a lot easier. I dragged the front half 100 feet then went back and dragged the back half and that's the way it went. On the last uphill stretch I could only go about 30 feet at a time and when I got to the top of the last stretch with the first half, I was one tired, happy guy. It was about 800 feet from there to my boat and all downhill but I still had to go back and drag the second piece up the last bit of hill.

All the time I was dragging the deer I remembered all the stories I've heard about old guys like me shooting a big buck and they find him later, lying by his big buck, dead of a heart attack. I had started dragging that deer about 10:20 a.m. and got to my boat with the two pieces at 3:20 p.m. By the time I got home, folks were organizing a search party to look for me. I knew while I was dragging that deer people would be wondering where I was, because most times I am back home by 1 p.m.

Living Off the Land and the Sea

I EAT A LOT OF SEAFOOD AND VENISON. MY FAVOURITE OF THE many cod species is the quillback rockfish. I fish for quillback a couple times a week and fillet them and put the fillets in the fridge overnight. If you don't refrigerate the fillets they will not lie flat when you go to fry them. When I cook them I dip the fillets in milk then roll them in flour and fry them in butter. I also like to deep-fry them in batter and the neighbours really like this, too, when I invite them for a fish and chip dinner.

The next best is the copper rockfish, which I prepare the same way. Yellow-eyed rockfish (red snapper) are good as long as they are not too big. They get coarse and tough when they are big. I eat kelp greenling, known as tommy cod, as well but we only eat the blue males. Many people don't like to bother with all the bones. There is a line of bones down the middle of the fillet and the way to deal with this is to take your knife and cut along each side of that line and remove the bones. They are a very mild and tender cod and best pan-fried in a bit of butter.

I like lingcod next best. Lingcod can be cooked a variety of ways. A 10- to 15-pound lingcod is the best eating, the flesh is fine and delicate, but the big ones can get tough and in the summertime they tend to get wormy.

Rock sole are a nice mild fish. You get four little fillets off one, which I put in the fridge overnight. I like to crush cracker crumbs and spread them on parchment paper on a cookie sheet, lay the fillets on the crumbs and sprinkle them on top as well. I mix together three tablespoons melted butter and one tablespoon each of French's prepared mustard, lemon juice and vinegar, and spread that over the fillets, then bake them in a hot oven for about ten minutes.

Sometimes I catch a grey cod and they are good but very soft and mild, the same as pollock. If you put a little bit of salt on the fillets and put them in the fridge for a day they will firm up.

I was told for years how good cabezon are but when I did catch one I was not impressed. I found its taste very strong and the flesh tough. My idea is, why eat something inferior when you can get the very best? I don't eat halibut if I can help it. I don't like the smell and find them very dry. If they are big they are tough. The best ones are about 30 pounds.

Sablefish (black cod) are delicious when smoked but are hard to catch because they live so deep, over 200 fathoms down. Herring are good and tasty but really have a lot of bones that are too hard to remove. Eulachon are a spring treat as they only come into the big rivers to spawn in March and April. I just roll them in flour and fry them.

I have never tried dogfish but did try ratfish, which tasted bad. Skate is alright but I don't like to kill one for the little bit of meat you get from it. They look like a prehistoric monster and taste a little bit like scallops.

Some of the best eating, of course, is salmon. I like pink and sockeye best. I will fish a pink salmon, boil some new potatoes when I get home, cut some steaks off the pink salmon and when the potatoes are almost done, place the steaks on top of the potatoes and boil for ten minutes. Drain off the water; eat with butter and salt and pepper.

Sockeye are done the same way but are best broiled with soy sauce and brown sugar. I will fillet a sockeye, remove all the bones and lay the fish on a cookie sheet. I put the soy sauce and sugar all over and let the fish marinate for a couple hours. Broil. Another way sockeye is good is to pan-fry steaks and eat them with strawberry jam. Sockeye are the best for canning. Don't add water, oil or salt, just can the salmon, bones and all.

I used to love to eat a winter spring but until just recently, I had not caught one in ten years. All spring salmon are good with their rich, oily flesh and they can be cooked many ways. I don't care for coho much as I find it very dry. Chum or dogs are poor to eat fresh but make real good smoked salmon.

When deer were plentiful and easy to hunt I always ate a lot. I love a venison roast. I cut holes into a small roast and poke pieces of garlic in, place a cut-up onion around the roast and bake it real slow. If I am going to have dinner at 5 p.m. I will put it in the oven at 140 degrees at 9 a.m. and turn the heat up to 350 for about forty-five minutes before I am ready to eat. Prepared this way the roast is always tender and tasty, never tough. I like to make venison stew and I boil the bones for soup stock. The rendered fat makes the most beautiful white fat and I use that for frying and making gravy. Venison burgers are great, too.

The best greens off the land are the nettles that grow all around my house. When they show their tiny green tips in March, I boil them lightly and eat them with butter, salt and pepper for a spring tonic. In the fall I make lots of jelly. I love to go up Wakeman Sound and get crabapples and make wild crabapple jelly; also salal berry jelly when the berries are dark purple and ripe.

Crab are good to eat and plentiful as well. The best way to eat crab is to boil them and then place a newspaper on the table and lay the crab out, clean and eat. Sometimes I dip the meat in

Digging clams for winter feeds at a beach near my home. Usually with the winter low tides this means digging in the dark. PHOTO BY YVONNE MAXIMCHUK

garlic butter. Prawns are good the same way but I like prawns best deep-fried in batter. I can a lot of crab because it is easy and quick to make a sandwich.

Some of the best winter eating is from butter clams, which I do not dig in the summer. You pick a dead low tide, which is usually on a pitch black night, and go out with lantern, clam fork and bucket. I like to take out the kids that visit Salmon Coast Field Station because most of them have never been out in the real dark and it is quite an experience for them. I hang the clams over the side of the dock for a few days so the sand gets cleaned out. I grind them up with onions, potatoes and carrots, garlic, bacon and a bit of milk for clam chowder, or make clam fritters. Littleneck clams are good steamed open and dipped in butter and garlic.

All this food from the land and the sea keeps down the grocery bills and I think has helped keep me healthy in more ways than one. I get lots of exercise going out and finding my food and it is very satisfying to go in the pantry and see jars of salmon, crab, jelly and other food so good and ready to eat.

CHAPTER FIVE

WILD ANIMALS AND STRANGE THINGS

Bambi the Tame Deer

IN 1954, THE GAME WARDEN BROUGHT A BIG BUCK DEER TO Freshwater Bay. He had him tied to the deck of the boat and he just came into shallow water and untied the buck and kicked him overboard.

There were lots of deer at Freshwater Bay, so why not one more? Well we soon found out why. The game warden had brought him to us and he turned out to be the biggest pest we had ever known.

The worst part was Mom loved him. To her he could do no wrong. That buck could open gates and he got so he could open doors too. He would come into the house and Mom would feed him bread or cookies. Mom smoked and he would clean out the ashtrays. One day he came in the house and jumped up on Mom's bed and peed. Mom was a bit mad at him that day, but still loved him. She always kept a big red ribbon on his neck and if he went away for a long time she would be out calling for him. Bambi used to sleep on a boat called *Seagull,* all curled up on the bunk, chewing his cud.

This went on for a year or so, then he started to swim out to Flower Island and out to Fresh Rock and Mom was sure someone

Mom would send me out to my boat to find Bambi, and when I did he would jump right in the boat. Ben Bachus and Elmer Pratt on the dock with Bambi at Freshwater Bay, about 1949. PHOTO BY JAE PROCTOR

was going to shoot him, so I would have to go bring him back home in my little outboard boat.

Before 1958, when I got my first chainsaw, I would cut all our firewood with a crosscut hand saw, and when you're sawing with a hand saw, they make a bit of a ringing sound. Bambi would hear that and come running. He would stand there watching me and when I pushed the saw through the cut he'd put his horns against the saw and bend it around and then jump back. There was no way I could saw when he was around.

Then he started to swim over to Bob Davies's place, and they were really scared of him. It seemed he did not like Mrs. Davies. I think it was because she was so scared of him, as all animals can smell fear. One day Bob brought him home on his boat and he had him tied to the deck cleat with a rope around his horns so his head was right down on the deck. I had to go and untie him and when I did, Bob climbed up on the wheelhouse roof.

One day Bambi came back with a big old jam can stuck on his horns and blood running all over his face. His horns were in the velvet and very sensitive and soft at this time. The can had cut off the end of one of his horns and I had to cut the can off with tin-snips. Luckily he was very calm and just stood there while I did this.

Bambi went away one day and never came back. We figured someone had probably shot him and we found out about a year later that was true: a guy had shot him swimming. So that was the end of Bambi.

Joey the Raccoon

WHEN I STILL LIVED ON A FLOAT IN THE BAY WHERE I LIVE NOW, Pierre Landry gave us Joey. He was just a small coon, but full of mischief. He kind of ruled the house and was always getting into some kind of trouble. He would go ashore to look around, then come and cry at the door wanting in. We would let him in and he would climb up on a chair and go to sleep.

Every afternoon after supper I would go and sit down on the sofa and eat some Smarties. As soon as Joey heard the Smarties box rattle, he would crawl up on my knee and beg for some. I would put a few in my hand and he would take one at a time and cover the rest with his little hand-like paw.

Anytime he got into bad trouble, he would go to my daughter Patty's bedroom and roll up in a comforter she had on her bed. This always happened whenever we caught him in the henhouse.

One day we got a call from the Echo Bay store to tell us Joey was over there getting into mischief, so Patty and I ran around and there was Joey with a bag of sugar down on the floor and he was licking it up. There were three big loggers in the store and they were scared of poor little Joey.

One guy said to Patty, "Watch out, he's real mean. He'll bite you." They were all staying clear of him. I paid for the bag of sugar and Patty went and picked up Joey. He just snuggled up to her.

Here's Joey; my daughter Patty doted on that little rascal. PHOTO BY BILL PROCTOR

Another day Patty took him out in the speedboat and he fell off the bow. The propeller hit him and made a small cut on his paw and broke a bit off one of his front teeth. Patty got him back in the boat and brought him home. As soon as he hit the dock he ran to the house and was crying at the door wanting in. My wife let him in and he went right to Patty's bed and rolled up in the comforter, crying like a little kid.

We had a big old boomstick tied to shore to hold the float-house off the beach and it had some four-inch holes in it. Joey would run ashore on the stick, but he always stopped at each hole to put in his little paw and see what he might find. Sometimes he would catch a little crab or a shrimp. When the tide went out, the end of the stick tied to the float would go underwater. He would have to swim to the float, but if anyone was looking he would stop at the edge of the water and start crying so one of us would come and get him.

As Joey got older he got a bit mean and would pick fights with any dog. I think one of the dogs at the school killed him because he went ashore one day and never came back.

We had our little pet raccoon for more than two years. He sure was a neat little pet and we missed him coming every afternoon looking for some Smarties.

The Great Horned Owl

FOR MANY YEARS WE HAD A DUCK POND AND I PUT A NET OVER it to keep the eagles and hawks from getting our ducks. One morning I went to feed the ducks and there was a great horned owl

Clack Clack, the Great Horned Owl, was a very gentle creature. PHOTO BY JAE PROCTOR

caught in the net. He looked pretty mad so I went for a pair of gloves and got him out. He had a small cut on one of his toes, so I carried him up and put him in a little shed we had. I made a roost for him to sit on, which he did right away.

At the time I was trapping mink. When I came back from trapping I always skinned the mink, so I cut some small pieces of meat and took them to feed to the owl. He was a bit shy at first but after he tasted a few pieces he just ate it all up. I did the same thing the next day and the next and after a few days, he started to clack his beak when I went to the shed. He came and sat on my arm. When I held out my hand with the meat in my palm he'd take a piece ever so gently until it was all gone and then clack his beak again. We called him Clack Clack.

I fed him like this for about a week and when his toe got all healed up I turned him loose in the forest. I hated to see him go. He was such an interesting, beautiful creature and so gentle.

Sea Monsters

IN AUGUST 1954 I WAS TROLLING IN BLACKFISH SOUND. IT WAS a flat, calm day; clear, bright and sunny. I was over by the White Rocks when I saw a big head sticking out of the water. It was around 800 feet from me, so I headed for it to see what it was. As soon as I turned toward it, it lifted its head up high out of the water. About six feet of it stuck up from the surface.

The creature had a head like a horse, about ten inches long. The neck was kind of flat and about eight inches thick. It looked like a giant cobra. I could see no body, just the head and what I took to be the neck. When I got about 200 feet from it, it sank and I never saw it again, but a friend of mine did. Chief Bill Scow packed clams in the area from November to April and he saw it near the White Rocks three times that year.

Another time I was running from Simoom Sound to Echo Bay in *Twilight Rock* when I saw what I took to be a big deadhead sticking out of the water, so I steered for it. There was about four feet of it sticking up. When I got close I could see it was a brown critter of some sort, about three feet across. It was just skin and no hair. When I ran alongside of it, it took off and kind of swam alongside of my boat. My boat was 37 feet long and this creature was just as long.

It dove down and I never saw it again. But around the same time there were more reports of people seeing what they called the "Log Thing." My neighbour Albert Munro saw it in Viner Sound and Jack Scott saw it out by the Burdwood Group.

Another day I was going to the Burdwoods in my speedboat. It was clear and flat calm. All of a sudden there were these big boils coming up in front of me, so I slowed down and when I got to that spot where the boils were, the boat fell about six inches into the trough this thing had made. I thought it must have been a whale, but I stopped and watched for quite a while and nothing ever came up.

Sasquatch Stories

IN 1979, MY BUDDY MEL BELVEAL AND I WERE ROWING UP THE Atah River in Bond Sound before daylight, to go goose hunting. We wanted to be hidden before daylight came.

I was sitting up above the oars, pushing forward with them, so I could see where I was going, and Mel was sitting in front of me, also looking ahead. I was rowing real quiet so as not to scare the geese. It was high tide and still dark, except for a little strip of light only about 10 feet wide down the centre of the river. The river at that point was about 100 feet wide. On the right side of the river were grass and cobble-sized rocks. The left bank was steep, with big trees, and covered in salal brush.

All at once we both heard something on the cobbles and we thought it was a bear. We could hear it go into the water. We got a glimpse of it when it crossed the little strip of light about 200 feet ahead of us.

The water at this point was four and a half to five feet deep. Whatever the creature was, it had to have been walking on the stream bottom, as it was going too fast to be swimming. We could see about four feet of it above the surface. When it got ashore we could hear it in the salal brush and it made a swell that rocked our rowboat.

I have seen a lot of bears in my time, but I have never seen one doing that across a river. If it was a bear, it would have had to have been running on two legs—which, generally speaking, bears do not do.

Another time I went deer hunting at the mouth of Thompson Sound, up an old skidder road. The road went back about a mile and a half and I knew there would be some big bucks right at the back end. I got in to shore and left the boat before daylight, as I wanted to get to the back end before the deer went into hiding for the day. The road was a bit steep and I was hiking as fast as I could. I had just got up the steep part to the flat part of the road by daylight.

The road went through a patch of young hemlock trees about 10 to 12 feet high on each side and I was walking swiftly along. I came around a bend in the road and stopped for a bit to look around. About 40 feet back in to the left side of the road I noticed the trees were shaking and swaying. There was no wind so this was a bit odd. Then I heard a *crack* and then another *crack* and I figured I must have scared a bear.

I still had a ways to go to where the big bucks lived so I kept going up the road. Well, I got to the back end and there were a lot of big buck tracks that were real fresh, but not a buck in sight, just some does. I turned back and when I got to where the trees had been shaking I went to see what it was that had been there.

When I got there, I first noticed several young hemlock trunks about seven or eight feet high, with the tops broken off. These hemlock tops had been laid side-by-side and formed a bed about four feet across by eight feet long. I could see where something had been lying down on the bed of hemlock tops. I wish I had looked around for some fur or other sign but the whole thing was so strange I just wanted to get out of there.

I have seen other mysterious things—such as a seven-inch footprint in Simoom Sound that was unlike any tracks I knew, and a UFO over Blackfish Sound—but these stories can be found in *Heart of the Raincoast*.

A Symbol of Life

THIS STORY MAY SEEM HARD TO BELIEVE BUT IT REALLY DID happen to me just the way I will tell it.

I had been trolling for salmon at La Pérouse Reef on the west coast of the Queen Charlotte Islands for six days and I was alone because I had not brought a deckhand. At night I would anchor behind Frederick Island and on the seventh day a gale of south-east came up, so at 2 p.m. I went in and anchored. This was not the best of anchorages so I watched carefully to be certain the anchor was holding. Once I felt sure that it was I went down below and lay down on my bunk, on top of the sleeping bag.

When you are in a situation like this you are in a state where you are resting deeply but still alert and aware of what is going on around you. So this is the way it was. I could hear the wind in the rigging and hear the anchor line as it came tight and I could feel when a gust of wind hit the boat. As I was lying there in this state I heard a new sound, a little foreign noise I never heard before, and I did not know what it was. I looked up the stairs into the galley and I saw a little object floating at the top of the stairs. There was a bit of mist, like halo around it.

Then I heard these words:

"This is a symbol of life and each outside window represents something that has happened or will happen in your lifetime. Seven of the windows are already used up so there are five left on the outside rim and the big one in the centre, which is the end of life."

The little object made a low whirring sound and then seemed to move out of my sight. As soon as it was gone I went upstairs and found some paper and drew what it looked like and wrote down what it said.

I could have sworn I was wide awake, but... ? I certainly was awake enough to write and draw what I saw and heard, but it is a hard thing to believe, even for me.

CHAPTER SIX
BILLY'S MUSEUM

Stone and Bone Tools

I OPENED MY MUSEUM ON JULY I OF 1999 BUT THE COLLECTING began sixty years ago at Freshwater Bay, where I found my first artifact while I was helping my mom in our garden. It was a jade chisel or skinning knife and I thought it was beautiful. I wiped the dirt off and held it in my hands and turned it over and over. After I found that jade piece I began to look around more, in the garden and on the shore, but two years passed before I found another piece, an arrowhead. Soon every time I went out looking I would find something. I got so I could spot the difference between a worked stone piece and a regular stone while just walking along a beach. I have never dug for artifacts; I just walk the beach at low tide and when I find one I always hold it in my hand and try to visualize what the person who made it might have looked like and what he or she might have been doing in their time. You can tell by some of the tools that some took real pride in their work. Others were not so nicely made; it makes me think people are not that much different today. I was interested in lots of other things too, including bottles and every other little thing that seemed to be going out of use or that turned up in some old camp garbage dump.

Stone arrowhead

I brought home so many items over the years I had to build shelves for them upstairs in our house. People would come and visit and go up to see the collection, and it just kept growing. So that was why I decided I'd better make a building for it all. I milled red cedar for the building and salvaged windows and I bought tin for the roof. I built display cases with glass covers to house the First Nations artifacts, shelves for the bottles and long counters for things like the post office items, business paperwork and records, brass bits and pieces I got off wrecked boats, and newspapers and marine magazines. I made the sign using pink fishing lures to spell out the words "Billy's Museum." Now, between April and October each year, three to four thousand visitors come to my museum, which kind of amazes me.

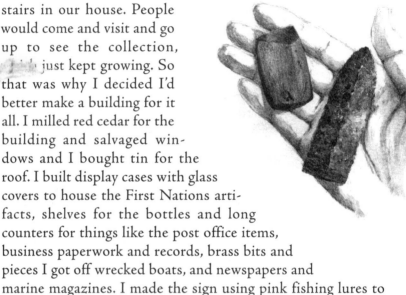

Stone arrowhead and jade skinning knife

Over the years the stone tools collection grew until I had axes, adzes and wedges, and a large number of arrowheads and spear points. Most of the spear points are carved or chipped from basalt but I've found six very striking points: three of chalcedony, which is a kind of marble, two made of obsidian and one of quartz crystal.

I've found old hide scrapers and some very old chipped knives; some are likely over five thousand years old and you can tell this by the roughness of the surface. The pieces were chipped away with

Thick spindle whorl and broken spindle whorl

harder stone, not sanded smooth. I found two spindle whorls, or fly wheels, which were put on a shaft to make a drilling tool. These are quite different from each other: one is larger and rough and the other is very fine and smoothly worked. The fine one was broken in two and I found the first piece and ten years later the second piece showed up on the same beach.

Once when I was anchored at Charles Creek in Kingcome Inlet I found a bear spear on the beach at low tide. This would have been lashed to a sturdy stick when in use.

PHOTO BY YVONNE MAXIMCHUK

Stone pestle and stone bear spear

On Lanz Island off Cape Scott I found some pestles when I was taking a shore break while out fishing one year. And out deer hunting in the fall once, I saw where a bear had been digging so I went to look. There, lying on top of the pile of dirt, was a real nice pestle, kind of a happy surprise. I also turned up two pebble tools on Lanz Island. Pebble tools were used to make other tools by "pecking," so they had to be made of real hard rock. I also have a good collection of hammer stones, which are just rocks that fit in the hand nicely and were used just like a hammer is today.

Rope making tool

A rope-making tool I found is kind of interesting. It has a hole in it that three strands of cedar bark fit through and you turn it to twist the bark into a rope. Lots of abrasion stones must have been made and used judging by the number I've found. These were used to sharpen tools and some are coarse and some are very fine like sandpaper today. One has a hole bored in one end; I think it was to carry it on a belt or around the neck.

Once I got a good eye for stone tools I realized there were plenty of bone bits lying around that had been shaped into a tool. It is pretty easy to find a deer bone needle and I have plenty. Also some bone spears and fish gorges, or toggle hooks, and one trolling hook. Bark beaters that were used to beat the cedar bark to make it soft were made of whalebone and I have found two over the years.

The other material used for tools was teeth; I have some teeth that were drilled for pendants and I think they are wolf and seal teeth. One of the prettiest things I ever found was a mussel shell pendant at Lanz Island and it is a real nice piece of jewelry.

A coastal collection is not complete without Japanese glass fish-

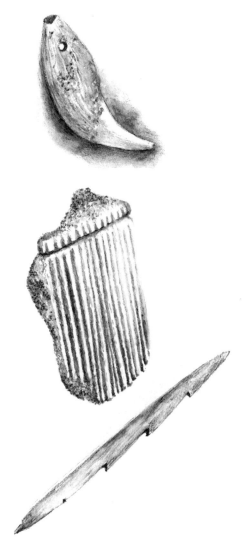

Top: Seal tooth pendant. Middle: Whalebone cedar bark beater. Bottom: Deer bone fish spear.

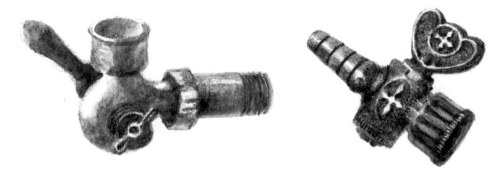

Bronze garden hose tap and brass priming cup

ing floats and my first find was a 10-inch one in Blackfish Sound, when I was ten years old. They come in many sizes and a few shapes. The rolling pin style is a bit rare, as is the "Dolly Parton," a double glass ball. You can also find brown glass floats that were blown locally out of beer bottles and were used on sunken gillnets to fish for dogfish.

I've always loved brass and bronze pieces. Whenever I am walking on the beach and I see a dirty, green piece of brass, I have to pick it up and bring it home and shine it up. I have oilers and grease cups, pressure relief valves off steam engines and a steam whistle. The beautiful brass piece on the museum's doorstep came off Walter Walters' boat *Iona*, and the clinometer came as a gift from Kevin Smith on the sailing ship *Maple Leaf*. There's a brass rudder stock cover off the steamer *Themis*, which sank on a reef at the mouth of Browning Pass off the north end of Balaclava Island. The binnacle compass is off my old boat *Dynamite II*.

Carburetors come in bronze, and I have one from a 1916 Studebaker car in Jennis Bay, a Schebler and Linkert carburetor off an Easthope engine and one off a Waukesha gas engine.

Trade Items

WHEN THE FIRST EUROPEAN TRAD-
ers came to the coast they brought
a lot of trade items with them and
one of the main items was beads. The
Europeans would trade beads for furs.
Most of these beads were glass and made in
Venice, Italy, and were traded worldwide.
The most numerous are the blue beads
and they were Russian. Amber beads
and the ones with white hearts were
Hudson's Bay beads. I was told that
Captain Vancouver traded the amber ones and Captain Cook traded
the round black ones.

Another major trade item, along
with firearms, was gun flints. I have
gun flints that I have found in various places that date back to the 1700s.

Gun flints

Hudson's Bay traded clay pipes as well and I've found many
stems but only one bowl. These pipes were made in Europe of
kaolin clay, which was also known as white earth. The Native
people made beads out of the broken pipe stem pieces.

Copper was another important trade item. The Native people
made nose rings and bracelets to wear. I've found numerous copper
bracelets. Some are old and made of thin rolled and hammered
copper, and others are just wire. I've also found a number of copper
needles. Animal traps were also a valued trade item and I have a
number of these, which were used to trap all fur-bearing animals.

Bottles

OLD BOTTLES WERE ANOTHER ITEM THAT I ALWAYS LOOKED FOR and collected. Bottle collecting is interesting because there are so many types, colours and shapes of bottles and they tell a story. I

found the first bottle in my collection while I was walking the beach on Davis Island. It was the first bottle I had seen that was embossed; it has "Northrop and Lyman Co." on one edge and "Canadian Hair Dye" on the other edge.

So that first bottle got me started as an avid bottle collector. Since that day I have collected over 1,300 bottles. After I had walked just about every beach in the area I began to ask the old-timers where there were old camps back in the woods. Whenever I had a minute of spare time I was out in the woods tracking down these old camps. I am pretty sure I have dug in every old camp in the Broughton Archipelago. Once I located a camp I would look around to see where the houses had been. In the old days people just opened the back door and threw everything out so that was always a good place to poke around. Usually there was a dump too, and when I found where the dump had been I would use a long rod to probe into the soil. When I hit glass I would dig. Often the bottle would be broken and I got some real bad cuts while digging. I used to carry a roll of tape to close up any cuts and keep right on digging.

A lot of bottles were patent medicine bottles, which was presented as a cure-all for everything. Some popular ones had mys-

Bottles and fresnel lenses from navigation lights on boats in the museum window.

PHOTO BY YVONNE MAXIMCHUK

terious sounding names... Fellows Syrup of Hypophosphites, Nuxated Iron, S.N. Thomas Eclectic Oil, Dr. Peter's Kuriko, Dr. Hostetter's Stomach Bitters, Dr. Davis Vegetable Painkiller, Dr. Chase's Syrup of Linseed and Turpentine. These medicines were guaranteed to cure just about everything, from colds to toothaches, constipation to diarrhea, grippe and pneumonia—the list goes on. The loggers would buy Dr. Davis Vegetable Painkiller by the case and mix it with lemon extract. I am pretty sure most of them had alcohol in them, which may have made it possible to swallow even Dr. Chase's Syrup of Linseed and Turpentine.

The glass is beautiful and some of the cosmetic jars and bottles were clearly designed to appeal to women. I have a vast collection of Avon bottles because there was always a woman who was the Avon Lady and the women in the camps bought lots of Avon creams and cosmetics. I found some hand and face cream bottles, two classic bath oil bottles and one demi-cup, all of milk glass, and Ponds cold cream and Arrid for Armpits jars. The blue bottles are some of the prettiest. Ones from Cod Liver Oil, Ayer's Hair Vigor, Milk of Magnesia, Nivea and Noxzema cream, and Vicks Vaporub all sit on shelves in the window.

It was pretty easy to find hundreds of beer bottles: quart Canadian beer bottles, embossed Vancouver and Victoria Brewers, and one beautiful amber bottle by Doering and Marstrand Brewing Co. Beer bottles came from China and Japan for loggers from there, and I found some Japanese sake and Chinese whiskey bottles too. Alcohol bottles include a half-pint-size Black Horse Ale, Guinness Stout and plenty of rum, gin (some of which are Dutch gin), wine and whiskey bottles.

Of course bottles have been good containers for cooking and food items for hundreds of years and I have plenty of canning

Various beer bottles from my collection in the museum. PHOTO BY YVONNE MAXIMCHUK

jars, dairy bottles and containers for ketchup, pickles, sauces and chutneys. Some containers are made of fired clay and these include Chinese soy sauce crocks and ginger pots, and one big brown gallon jug. Some of the most interesting bottles are the tiny, delicate opium bottles imported by the Chinese.

I organized the booths or areas in the museum so everything was easy to see. One section has household items that were used every day in the home. There's a Coleman gas iron and another iron that had to be opened and filled with hot coals to heat it, which both must have been pretty challenging to use. A few sad irons that sat on the stove to get warm, plus wash boards, meat grinders and a hand wringer for washing—all aids for the woman of the house to help her with her daily toil.

For the men, there was an assortment of hand tools such as the crosscut saw, broad axe, spoke shave, draw knife, soldering irons, blowtorches, hand planes, double-bitted axes and other odds and ends. Most of these items are now all electric. There is a lot to be said for hand tools. They were well made and usually did not break down and could be used anywhere, whether a man had a generator or not.

I have a big section for fishing gear, much of which has been described elsewhere, but it is all quite interesting. I have everything we used to need to make spoons; the wooden form and little round hammer, the sheets of spoon metal, lead moulds for pouring cod lures. Cedar gillnet corks and seine corks, many types of old spoons and flashers and plugs. I have some cannonballs made of cast iron instead of lead, because during World War II all lead was used to make ammunition for the war effort, so cast iron was substituted.

After I built the main museum building, people gave me a few more things plus I had all the parts of a blacksmith shop. The next summer I made a building with two rooms, one for a gift shop and one for the forge, and the following year I added another room to the main museum. The forge includes a complete set of tongs, melting ladles and a swage block, or shaper. I fired it up one day and it works just fine.

I also have a two-speed self-feed post drill, a Pionjar gas-powered rock drill and a climber's belt and spurs. Other items in with the forge are a Fairbanks Morse steam fire pump, blowtorches, carbide lamps and a rail bender. There's a good collection of old logging equipment, a 1948 Hornet chainsaw and a 1951 Disston with a six-foot bar. Lots of rigging, such as guy line shackles, moving blocks, tree plates, high lead block hand winches and an authentic "gut hammer" (triangular dinner bell) that kids like to ring. It's loud.

A few years later I found out about the metal remains of a shake sled lying way back in the woods near Greenway Sound. Horses would haul the sled, loaded with shake blocks, out of the woods on a specially built roadway. The sled timbers were all rotten but the hardware was good, so with the help of a friend I packed it all down to the beach. I took everything home and cleaned up all the rusted pieces, cut new timbers to fit, built 30 feet of road and set up the sled on it as a replica of the real thing. I have a can of skid grease, too; with that and a brush, a guy would have gone along painting grease on the roadway to make the sled slip along easier.

The shake sled I found in Greenway Sound and restored. PHOTO BY YVONNE MAXIMCHUK

The Hand Logger's Shack

WHEN I WAS A BOY THERE WERE A LOT OF HAND LOGGERS IN the area and many of them lived in little shacks along the shores of the inlets and sounds. I poked around in some of these shacks years ago and I noticed how they were built, so in 2010 when I felt I needed a new project I decided to build one to show people a bit of the hand logger's life.

Through the years I have split a lot of cedar for roofs and fences. For anyone who has never done this I will try to explain how it is done. My shack is 10 feet by 10 feet, which was the size of most of the hand loggers' shacks. I wanted to make my replica as close as possible to the real thing. I used only a hand saw, a claw hammer, a sledge hammer, steel splitting wedges, a froe and yew wood club, and a bench axe—no level or square or power tools—so I could make it the same way the old-timer hand loggers had.

First you need three small logs 10 feet long and 8 to 10 inches in diameter, which you lay parallel to each other as level as possible

Interior of the hand loggers shack showing the simple bed and furniture the hand loggers used. I built everything with hand tools, like the old hand loggers did.
PHOTO BY YVONNE MAXIMCHUK

for the foundation. Next you'll need a floor and for this you need a log at least 2 feet in diameter and a little over 10 feet long so you have some left over for trim; the bigger the log the better. The log will have to be split in half lengthwise and for this you will need two good, thick split-ting wedges made of steel and a 10-pound sledgehammer. You take one wedge and use it to tap in a half-inch line straight across the centre of the log. The line must be straight and unbroken all the way across the heart of the log because when you go to split the log, the split will follow this line.

Hand winch and shackle lie below the steps up to the hand loggers shack. PHOTO BY YVONNE MAXIMCHUK

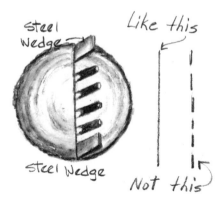

You drive one wedge in near the outer edge of the log and the other wedge in the other side. Once you have both wedges in as far as they can go, you take the bench axe and use it to make a bunch of wooden wedges. You will make the wedges a little larger than the size of the crack. Use a 2-inch cedar limb and cut several pieces about 12 inches long and shape the ends into wedges. It is better to cut these with the bench axe rather than a chainsaw because the ones cut with the chainsaw tend to be rough and will stick when you try to drive them in.

Take four of these wedges and drive them in the crack that has opened up across the end of the log; put them all in one after the other and tap each in just a little at a time, because if you hit one more than another the wedge might split. You have to keep even pressure on the wedges. If the log doesn't want to split easily put in more wedges between the ones you already have in. Right about now the split should be open about an inch and a half and the crack will be opening along the side of the log, so you take more wooden wedges and drive them in along that crack. When you get these wedges in the first ones on the end should fall out.

At this point you must block the log to stop it from rolling, because sometimes a log will split very fast and the side beside which you are working could roll on you. Tap the wedges in until the log splits all the way down and the half rolls away from you. So now you have the log in half, you must split the halves in half and you do this the same way, by marking a line across the centre with the steel wedge. The halves should split easily. Now you will have four quarters and you are ready to split planks for the floor. These should be about 2 inches thick and as wide as they will split. Mark the line with the steel wedge and use the wooden wedges the same way, to split the planks. Remember the split will always follow the line you mark.

For a 10 x 10 shack you need about twelve or fourteen planks for the floor. You'll need 4-inch nails to nail the planks to the support logs you already have in place. Never leave any sap wood on the planks or on shakes because it will rot quickly. So you take the bench axe and trim off the sap wood and any bumps so the planks fit together tightly. This can take a bit of time. Just lay each plank down against the previous one and you will see where it needs to be trimmed.

Now split the rest of the 10-foot block into 2-inch planks and then split these planks as close as you can into 2 x 4 lengths for the studs and rafters. It doesn't matter if they are not exact; they might be 3 x 3 or 2 x 3. Take four of these 10-foot lengths and nail them down around the perimeter of the floor. Sometimes these are not perfectly straight but as you nail them down you can eyeball them and straighten them out. Once all four are nailed down, take your hand saw and trim off any ends of the floor planks that stick out beyond the 2 x 4s so you end up with a straight face to nail the shakes to.

Next you will need a standard 4-foot-diameter shake block for shakes, studs and braces. So once again you make a line across the block with the wedge, split it in half and then into quarters.

At this point you might ask, "Why did we stop putting up the frame and go start splitting the shake block?" My answer is you already have 2 x 4s but they are all 10 feet long and you don't

want to cut these long ones because you will
need them later.

This is what the end of the block looks like.

So take a wedge and split the heartwood
out. It is no good for shakes but you can make 2
x 4s out of it and shakes out of the outside. Start
splitting 2 x 4s (or 2 x 2s or 2 x 3s; it doesn't matter)
from the heartwood; you will need eight studs 3 feet 2
inches long, so cut the length with your hand saw.

With the bench axe, flatten off the 2 x 4 where the stud is going
to sit on the 2 x 4 that is already nailed down around the outside
edge of the floor. Stand the 2 x 4 up as straight as you can on the
flat spot and toenail it in place with 2 ½-inch shake nails. Do this
in each of the three spots along the wall. Now take one of the 10-
foot 2 x 4s and nail it across the top of the three studs, with 4-inch
nails. As you nail this in place make sure the studs are as straight
as you can eyeball. Now you will need fifteen braces and you can
use any of the 4-foot pieces that were not thick enough to be good

I constructed the framing in two sections,
the lower one first, then the upper one.
PHOTO BY YVONNE MAXIMCHUK

Here you can see the corner
detail with the bracing pieces.
PHOTO BY YVONNE MAXIMCHUK

for studs. Take a brace and place it at an angle between the bottom and up to near the top of the vertical stud. Mark the angle on it and cut it to the size you marked. Sometimes you will have to flatten the spot where the brace is going to be. You use the 2 ½-inch nails to nail the brace to the bottom stud and upright stud.

Now you might wonder, "Why so many braces?" This is because some of these shacks were built in very windy places like Wakeman Sound or Tribune Channel. The hand logger needed a sturdy house that would not fall down around him. After fifty years, some of them were still standing and only recently have they finally collapsed.

Now that you have the bottom section of the framing in place you need some shakes, so you go to the remaining quarters and start to split the shakes. You will need a froe for this and a hard wooden club. I have heard that some folks use a ten-pin bowling pin as the club but I made my own club out of yew wood.

To make a half-inch-thick shake, stand the froe on the block with the blade down and hit it with the club. The big secret is to hold the froe very still as you hit it. This is very important as it will help you make the shakes nice and even. Drive the froe in until the blade is flush with the top of the block, then tip it toward yourself, shove it down and tip it again. With 4-foot shakes you likely have to tip the froe three or four times, depending on how easily the block splits.

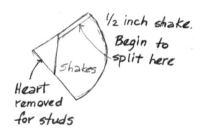

½ inch shake.
Begin to split here

Shakes

Heart removed for studs

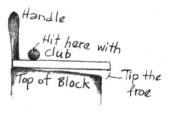

Handle

Hit here with club

Top of Block

Tip the froe

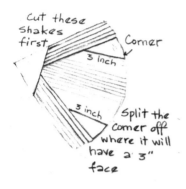

Cut these shakes first

Corner

3 inch

3 inch / Split the corner off where it will have a 3" face

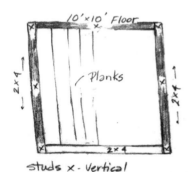

10' x 10' Floor

Planks

2×4

2×4

2×4

Studs x - Vertical
2×4 - Horizontal on planks

Here is a tip: wet wood splits easier than dry wood. If you have a real dry log, pour some water on the block. I like to split shakes when it is raining. On a wide shake you really have to hit the froe hard and it can help if you tip up the far end of the froe blade just a bit.

When you get these shakes cut, split off the corner where it will have a 3-inch face. You do this so your shakes will be edge grain.

You split shakes until your arm is sore and then you nail them on. I always lay them down "barn" fashion. This makes a double row nailed down on both ends, which prevents the shakes from curling up or leaking. Nail down shakes on the short wall you built on top of the floor. When you put the first shake up, put one nail in the top to hold it in place. Nail up the rest of the shakes along the wall. Then you put on the top layer and make sure it overlaps the first layer by at least an inch and a half beyond the seam. Use two nails in the top and two in the bottom, unless the shake is quite wide, in which case use three nails across. Lay up shakes around the whole building except where your door will be.

Now you are ready to put on the top half of the wall and you repeat the steps with 2 x 4 studs and a 10-foot-long 2 x 4 across the top. You'll need eight more studs and fifteen more braces, then three or four ceiling joists, which also must be 10 feet long. After you get the top wall section covered with the shakes you can start on the roof, and then lay the ceiling joists across from one wall to the other.

The length of your rafters will depend on how steep you make the roof. You'll need ten rafters and some studs for the gable ends, and a ridge pole that also must be 10 feet long. Allow for at least 14 inches extra for the eaves. Once you get the rafters up you'll need strapping to nail the roof shakes to. For this you can use 10-foot studs along with some of the 4-footers because the strapping must be 13 feet long to allow for overhang on the ends. The short pieces are easily joined in by nailing them to the rafters.

Once you get the rafters up you are ready to deal with the strapping and the shakes. For the roof it is best to make the shakes 2 feet long. They are easier to split and make for a better roof. Make sure your strapping is the right distance apart to nail the shakes to. You can set the strapping in place as you get ready to nail down the shakes. When you are nailing down the roof shakes, be sure to leave a quarter-inch between each shake, and when you

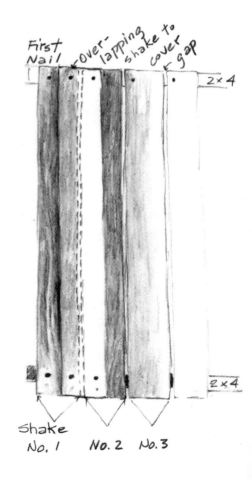

First Nail

overlapping shake to cover gap

2 × 4

2 × 4

Shake No. 1   No. 2   No. 3

put on the second layer be sure to place the second shake so it fully covers the gap by at least 2 inches. Layer each row of shakes with 3 inches overlapping the one beneath it and put two nails in each end.

If you have made it this far, you will probably be able to fashion a door and a window on your own.

I know you are going to ask, "Why not use store bought 2×4s and 1×4 strapping?" You can if you want, but then it is not an authentic hand logger's shack. I'll be interested to hear if anyone is able to build a hand logger's shack from these directions.

MY MUSEUM COLLECTION IS KIND OF LIKE A THREE-DIMENsional encyclopedia. There are so many different items in it that can teach us about what life was like thousands of years ago,

Fishing gear section inside my museum with the hand-loggers shack visible through the window. PHOTO BY YVONNE MAXIMCHUK

hundreds of years ago and right up to the present day. There is something that shows just about every activity that might have been done by a person at any moment from now right back into the mists of time.

IN OCTOBER 2014, SCHOOL DISTRICT 85 MADE A DECISION TO tear down, destroy and burn Echo Bay School and all the contents from the school that had not been previously removed or sold to members of the Echo Bay community. No warning was given and little effort was made by the school board to remove or transfer items (such as desks, chairs, printers and computers, power switch boxes, propane heaters, toilets, sinks, etc.) to other schools or to where they might be put to use. Lying around on shelves were boxes of paper, thousands of books and teaching aids, and various items that formed a historical record of at least some of the generations of students and teachers and their accomplishments.

Billy noticed the noise and activity on one of his many walks and alerted community members. A few of us were able to salvage some items of actual monetary and functional value and I was able to salvage a lot of material of historical value, including photographs and newsletters. Billy managed to save the piano; it was out of tune and unused for many years, but he had brought it in to the school back in the '70s on *Twilight Rock*.

All that remains now are the white shell scars where the schoolhouse sat and was burned, the track through the midden on the beach where the trailer was yarded out to a barge and a few incompletely burned books, CDs and toys. Even the swing set was decreed a liability problem and could not be re-situated in Echo Bay Provincial Marine Park.

I built the original Billy's Museum (left) in 1999 and the gift shop with the B/A (British American) oil company sign (right) was built in 2000. The schoolhouse is a new addition in 2015 and can be seen under construction in the centre. PHOTO BY YVONNE MAXIMCHUK

A couple of weeks later Billy told me about his next museum project. He would build a little schoolhouse, to house the things we had managed to save and to have it to remember an important part of the history of the area. His project for early 2015 became the salvage (a favourite activity!), from local sinking shacks, of all the materials he needed for the framing, windows, roofing and inside finishing. His only actual purchase was milled cedar for the siding, so the building will be beautiful. Inside the little schoolhouse, situated beside the hand logger's shack, next summer's visitors will find the bits and pieces we salvaged—testament, once again, to the end of an era.

FINALE

Listening to the Universe

I BELIEVE WE SHOULD ALWAYS LISTEN TO WHAT THE UNIVERSE is trying to tell us, but sometimes we neglect to do this and we get into a bit of a jackpot... meaning trouble, in this case. But if we listen, everything just falls into place. I will give you a few examples of some things that have happened to me by heeding what the universe has told me.

On August 13, 1958, I was fishing for sockeye in Blackfish Sound and was doing really well, but I was restless. I had been told Cockatrice Bay was a good place to catch big spring salmon but I had never even been there before and I was not exactly sure where it was. I got my chart out and found where it was, picked up my gear and headed off to Cockatrice Bay. When I got there I put out my spring salmon gear, all Wonder spoons, and I trolled into the bay. Right away I began to catch springs and I ended up with twenty-one large salmon, the smallest of which was 38 pounds and the largest 42. They looked like they had all been made in the same mould.

When I got back to the camp that night I found out that the sockeye fishing had dropped off that afternoon.

Another day I was fishing pinks in Blackfish Sound and not doing very well. I got a strong feeling to go fish the bank in Baronet Pass, so I pulled the gear and ran down there. That night I went into camp with a deckload of pinks, sockeye and coho, and a few big springs.

In 1956 I wanted to go and fish offshore so I needed a bigger boat. There was a big boat for sale in Sointula, *Fisher Boy*. It was just what I was looking for but it cost $10,000, and I didn't have $10,000. I needed a loan so I went to ABC Packing, the company I had sold all my fish to up to that point. They told me they would not make a loan to a troller.

Then I went to BC Packers and they did not know me, so no loan from them. Finally I went to a friend at Alert Bay Shipyards and in October he loaned me most of the money.

Well, that turned out to be the biggest mistake I ever made in my lifetime. The boat was old and rundown and I had nothing but problems with it. I fished it one season and sold it and went back to a smaller boat, *Dynamite II*. If I had listened to the universe, i.e. paid attention to the difficulty I had in getting a loan, I never would have bought that boat.

I fished that small boat for sixteen years and it was good to me. Then I decided to have a boat built in Vancouver, which I named *Twilight Rock*, and I fished that boat for the next twenty years. One day in 1993 I went to Port McNeill; I had no intention of selling my boat when I left home but when I got to town I put a "Boat For Sale" sign on the billboard at the top of the ramp. Before I even got home a man phoned me on the radio wanting to buy *Twilight Rock*, but I told him I had to find another boat before I sold it.

For over twenty years I'd wanted to get a Morris Gronlund boat, the boat of my dreams. I found out a Morris Gronlund boat, *Ocean Dawn*, was up for sale. Later I learned it had been put up for sale at almost the same hour I had put the "Boat For Sale" sign up at the Port McNeill dock.

My boat, Ocean Dawn, *tied to the float in Port Hardy in 1995, the first year I fished her, with Yvonne Maximchuk deck-handing for me.* PHOTO BY YVONNE MAXIMCHUK

These kinds of things happen when we listen to the little voice in our heads. When you don't heed that little message—some call it intuition—things just don't work out the way they should.

INDEX

Bold entries refer to illustrations, maps and photos